Colossal Christ:

The Preeminence and All-Sufficiency of Jesus in the Christian Life

Ken Marino

Colossal Christ: The Preeminence and All-Sufficiency of Jesus in the Christian Life
First printing: March, 2016

Edited by Rick Gallipeau
Cover design by Jeff Sullivan/Sullivan Designs
Cover image by iStock by Getty Images/Andrew Mayovskyy

Printed in the United States of America
Printed by CreateSpace, An Amazon.com Company
ISBN-13: 978-1530713486 (Paperback edition)
ISBN-10: 153071348X (Paperback edition)

This book is dedicated to Edward P. (Ed) Miller, whose teachings have been a powerful influence on me by blending diligent scholarship with the indispensable principle of Bible study—absolute, total reliance on the Holy Spirit. Ed's contagious passion in seeing Jesus Christ in the Bible has been a priceless gift from the Lord to me.

Contents

Preface

The greatest treatment on the *how* of holiness in all the New Testament, in my opinion, is found tucked away in the not-so-frequented book of Colossians. While all the books of the Bible reveal different aspects of the holiness of God—for God is holy—Colossians presents Jesus Christ as the universe, the all in all, of our holiness unlike any other. I'd like to invite you along an extraordinary journey to discover with me these stupendous truths from Colossians. Understanding the Holy Spirit's intent for this colossal revelation of Christ will free you from your flesh and produce the fruits of righteousness as never before. We live in an information age of amazing technological advances. Yet as sin is abounding, where is grace much more abounding? If you find yourself in a spin cycle of sin and temptation, discouraged about ever being free, take heart, dear brother or sister in Christ. You have great news ahead of you! A faithful band of brothers and sisters have struggled over these very same issues and found release from their captivity through the heaven-sent message that Paul delivered to them.

Indian mystic and missionary Sadhu Sundar Singh, in his arduous travels across the Himalayas, encountered a hermit holed up in a dark cave. This old Buddhist lama in his quest for spiritual advancement had built a stone wall at the entrance, leaving only a small opening for air, through which benevolent villagers passed in barley and tea. Having lived for so many years in the inky darkness, he eventually went blind. The hermit lamented, "I live in spiritual darkness. I do not know what the end will be, but I am sure that whatever I now lack will be attained in another life."[1]

I know what it's like to have lived in that cave. Like the old Buddhist lama, I was a zealot for the spiritual advancement I read about in the Bible and heard preached from the pulpit. I worked my head off to battle against the three great obstacles to my progress in holiness: my sin-tainted flesh, the ever-present temptations in this secular world, and Satan, that unseen prince of darkness. Yet for all this, I commiserated with the lama's lament that my lack could only be attained in another life, in heaven's sweet by and by. In my religious zeal, I had unwittingly stone-walled the light of the Lord Jesus as my all in all to but a very small aperture. My approach to the Bible lacked the superior centrality of Christ I needed to overcome the flesh, the world, and the devil and exhibit His love and life.

For over fifteen years, my Christian journey consisted of meager portions of Christ with bounteous helpings of church busyness, over 25 meetings a month—services, prayer meetings, small group meetings, young adult meetings, evangelistic outreach activities, and more. I sincerely believed that my wholehearted participation in all these activities would accelerate my progress on my quest to be like Jesus. Like many of my friends and people I looked up to, I

[1]Benge, Janet & Geoff, Sundar Singh: Footprints Over the Mountains (Seattle, WA: YWAM Publishing, 2005), pp. 148-149

thought, *I have yucky flesh and live in a yucky world, so I need to keep super busy with church activities to stay out of trouble and be holy.* It was during my twilight time that God mercifully began to dawn on my heart the wonderful revelation from Colossians that set me free: the preeminence of Jesus!

Can you identify at all with my struggle? Do you find that your Christianity is filled with many distractions and non-essentials that shut up the light of Jesus Christ Himself? Do you find elusive the one thing needful, sitting at Jesus' feet like Mary, and are you worried and troubled like Martha, distracted by your many Christian activities, meetings, and services? If ever there was a day when the message of the book of Colossians was needed, that day is today. My heart goes out to the many brothers and sisters captive to the abounding sins of our culture, whose deep lacerations in the soul need the healing of Christ that Colossians offers. Have you resigned yourself that whatever you now lack, like that despondent Himalayan lama, will just have to be attained in another life—heaven? The book of Colossians trumpets a liberating message: let the stone wall of our cave fall down and allow the full blaze of the glory of the Lord to shine forth into our inky darkness!

This book you hold in your hands is first and foremost about the preeminence of Jesus Christ as our hope of glory in this cruddy world. It was born from above in my heart as a milestone along my spiritual journey almost a decade ago. The seed of this book began in December of 2005 when I met up several late night Fridays with a friend, Scott Shelton, for spontaneous, unhurried times of seeking and worshiping the Lord Jesus. We were both just hungry for God and longing for a move of His Spirit on us and our church.

How God over-answered that prayer! In early 2006 the Lord directed me, via the Internet, to the teaching ministry of Ed Miller of Bible Study Ministries out of Rhode Island. As I listened intently to each message, I became increasingly amazed at how every book in the Bible had a unique revelation of the Lord Jesus Christ.

Colossians was the first book the Lord opened up to my heart in a real way during my own personal studies, and I've never been the same. I devoured any audio series on Colossians on the Internet and any written resource I could get my hands on. In 2010 God used an audio series on Colossians by Tullian Tchividjian, a popular gospel-centered preacher, to motivate me to assemble in a book the rich truth He gave me of the preeminent Christ.

Since then, I have been attending a Bible conference at a Christian retreat center near Lancaster, Pennsylvania. I sent a few soft copies of the book to a few like-hearted brothers. When I came up to the spring men's retreat in 2011, Ed Miller greeted me and asked me with what seemed to me a stunned expression on his face and asked, "Have you considered publishing this book?" The question took me aback. I really hadn't seriously thought about it. Fast forward now to 2016 and my heart is still keen on the preeminence of Jesus Christ in my life. Although the original material has undergone an extreme makeover since then, I trust by God's grace that the unveiling of Christ that resonated in Ed's heart is still faithfully portrayed in this new and revised edition.

Recorded Bible study sessions I taught at my workplace back in 2010 to a handful of brothers helped to fill in some big content gaps from Colossians 2, 3, and 4.

2 Kings 6 and 7 tell the story of four lepers who stumbled into tremendous wealth at a time when the northern kingdom's capital city of Samaria was greatly distressed because of a long siege by the Syrian army. It was so bad that donkey heads and dove dung were being sold at exorbitant prices. As these four men ventured out to the Syrian camp, they were amazed to find it deserted but laden with abandoned tents and horses, food and drink, and gold and clothing. At first they desired to keep all this wealth to themselves, but then it dawned on them, "We are not doing what is right. This day is a day of good news, and we remain silent." This lavish wealth was too much to keep to themselves; they had to share it. I have often felt humbled that the Lord would grant such lavish riches of understanding and seeing Christ in Colossians. I discharge this burden by sharing this "day of good news."

I have written this book with the average Christian in mind. Though we'll investigate the grand themes of Colossians and even at times dip down into the original Greek text, you don't need to be a scholarly theologian to get it. I intentionally used simple, common language to help you understand God's heart without "dumbing it down" or getting lost in the technical jargon of a PHD dissertation. Wherever possible I used simple everyday analogies as windows that let the light in upon some of the more challenging ideas. Yet for all this, even our best explanations need the illumination of the Holy Spirit, the capital A author of Colossians. It is my prayer for you, dear reader, "that the God of our Lord Jesus Christ, the Father of glory, may give you the Spirit of wisdom and of revelation in the knowledge of him" (Ephesians 1:17 ESV).

My daughter, Cayla, is now bored with perhaps the most epic saga that has enthralled American culture for the past forty years: Star Wars (excluding the recently released number 7 that she saw only once). Her younger brothers just watched it too many times. By contrast, despite having pored over the words of Colossians countless times, my excitement about Jesus in it only continues to grow. The presence of the Holy Spirit ignites a fire in my soul to see Jesus better. So I humbly offer these insights freely given me, that the reader may emerge from the dark cave of frustration, struggle, discouragement, and doubt with the Christian life and into the blazing light of this colossal Christ who desires to manifest His glorious preeminence at all times.

Part 1

Diagnosing Doubt and Discouragement: Amnesia in a Jesus Universe

CHAPTER 1

Concentrating on the Light

Much of our stagnation and frustration in the Christian life can be traced back to one root problem: we don't pay close enough attention to Jesus Christ Himself. Colossians is a power-packed epistle that addresses the root of discouragement in our lives, a downheartedness stemming from falling short of God's glory in our day-to-day existence. The dilemma facing the Colossian church—and perhaps with greater intensity in our day—is superbly illustrated by the following excerpt from one of my all time favorite chapters in Fawn Parish's book called *It's All About You Jesus*:

> No one figured he'd amount to much. He was scrawny, the kind of kid other kids make sport of mocking. He was a decidedly unhurried learner. School bored him. A terrible test taker, he was eight before he could read. Unexpectedly, he ended up finding a seat at history's table. He made history by making one incredible decision. Augustin Jean Fresnel's life is more than just a great story,

a curious paradox, a tale with unexpected twists and turns. Augustin's decision has immense significance for every lover of God.

Sailors' lives in Augustin's day were routinely endangered. Lighthouses could not project light out to sea far enough to warn oncoming ships. Ship captains often didn't see the light until it was too late to change course. Skeletons of rotting ships littered the beaches of the world. The problem was not for lack of well placed lighthouses, but for lack of light being reflected far enough out to sea to penetrate the darkness.

For two thousand years people explored ways to correct the problem, finding little success. Starting with the lighthouse of Alexandria built around 280 BC, until the 18th century, lighthouses saw very little improvement in their ability to project light. It wasn't because people weren't trying. Most concentrated on developing better fuel. People thought if they could just make the flame brighter, it would solve the problem. Wood, coal, whale lamps, nothing proved effectual. The breakthrough came two thousand years later, when Augustin Jean Fresnel decided to take a different course. Instead of trying to improve existing lighthouse technology, or producing better fuel, Fresnel would study the behavior of light itself.

Fresnel didn't study lighthouses. He did not focus on design, maximum configuration, and placement. He wouldn't exhume the ribs of fractured ships and do a doctoral thesis on flawed ship construction. He never designed a manual on lighthouse maintenance and staffing. Instead (and this is the crucial point of this book), he spent his life studying light itself...and for thousands of ships and sailors, that made all the difference.

Fresnel, using the properties of reflected light, built an apparatus that could be seen from more than 20 miles away. His studies in light became the principle used in headlights of cars and in the flashing lights on police and emergency vehicles. By studying the behavior of light itself, Fresnel developed a lens that could reflect light far out to sea. Fresnel grew up to become the father of modern optics. His story illustrates a compelling reality for the people of God. It is more meaningful to study the character of Light Himself, than to concentrate on any the other thing related to Him.

We face the same problem faced in Fresnel's day. We have light, glorious light, but it isn't reflected far enough out to sea. Lives, marriages, and institutions daily land shipwrecked and sundered, bleached and rotting on our shores; yet we persist in tending the light, hoping to warn a few ships to turn toward deeper waters.

The Light is not, nor will ever be, insufficient to penetrate the darkness. Jesus is completely and utterly sufficient. But He has chosen to be magnified through the lens of our lives. We are reflecting Him poorly, because we are not focused on Him. We need more Augustins who will concentrate themselves solely on knowing light. Our greatest need is simplicity of devotion to Jesus. We're aware that countless ships are colliding in the night. We know the statistics. We've seen the skeletons on our beaches. The children of Light must be concentrated on Light Himself. We are concentrating on many things related to Him, but we are not focused primarily on Him. The main thing is no longer the main thing. Or perhaps I should say, the main One is no longer the main One.[2]

---

[2]Fawn Parish, *It's All About You Jesus* (http://www.reignbridge.com/?page=iaayj retrieved on December 28, 2007), used by permission

My hope, in this study of Colossians, is to avoid the shipwrecks of lives, marriages, and institutions by shining the Light, the Lord Jesus Christ, farther out to sea. "The children of Light must be concentrated on Light Himself." As we lay hold of God's remedy for the real problem these real believers were facing, we will find Jesus utterly sufficient for every area of our lives. He is truly all we need. Colossians gets our focus upon the Light, the Lord Jesus, in a way that maximizes spiritual growth.

Our tour guide, Paul, has guided our alpine itinerary through the book of Colossians to mount up from wonder to jaw-dropping wonder in the person and work of the Lord Jesus Christ. He leads us onward to the breathtaking implications of the historical facts of Christ's death, resurrection, and ascension to the right hand of the Majesty. Paul yearns to instruct the saints in a fuller understanding of what God has done, is doing, and will do for us in Christ. It is to our great loss that we overlook, by too cursory a glance, the treasure-filled palaces of Christ in the word of God. We *see* but have not *observed* them. A. W. Tozer poignantly perceived,

> May not the inadequacy of much of our spiritual experience be traced back to our habit of skipping through the corridors of the kingdom like little children through the market place, chattering about everything but pausing to learn the true value of nothing?[3]

Colossians is a kingdom corridor showcasing the breathtaking glories of the Lord Jesus Christ in His

---

[3] A. W. Tozer, "Tozer Devotional: Give Time to God" (http://www.cmalliance.org/devotions/tozer?id=178 retrieved on April 5, 2011)

preeminence in the entire created universe. We want to pause long enough in this hallowed hall to allow the true value of Christ to soak into our hearts and minds. This brings God glory! Dr. Charles J. Rolls, renowned in his day for his encyclopedic knowledge of Scripture and his radiant devotion to the Lord Jesus Christ, made this observation:

> Christians in general spend far too little time investigating the incomparable glories of this peerless Christ. There are many today who have but a poverty-stricken estimate of Him.[4]

We as Christians too often have lived in the filthy squalor of the flesh when in fact we are the rightful heirs of the incalculable riches of the Godhead.   Truly, the incomparable glories of Jesus Christ are meant to enrich even the most spiritually impoverished among us. A wide-eyed vista of the colossal Christ is what holds out hope for the downcast Christian.   Paul ransacks all creation for supreme metaphors to assure us that we have been firmly planted into the Lord Jesus Christ and His unshakeable kingdom. The Holy Spirit yearns to apply the brushstrokes of these sublime portraits of Christ upon the canvas of our faith. Through the Spirit's illumination we enter into the wonderland of a Christ who is all we need for the Christian life. But this is no never-never land fairy tale which vanishes into thin air. This is the ever growing paradise of faith in our Lord Jesus that will amaze us through all eternity!

---

[4] Charles J. Rolls, *The Indescribable Christ: Names and Titles of Jesus Christ A - G* (Neptune, New Jersey: Loizeaux Brothers, 1983), p. 38

Why Study Colossians?

About nine years ago the Lord impressed very deeply on me to study the book of Colossians as a whole and not as disconnected pieces. I was clueless that God had a simple theme around which all the complex ideas cluster. The one unifying theme reveals from beginning to end the Lord Jesus Christ in a way that no other book in the Bible does. What I discovered from this investigation sparked a mighty transformation in my life. I began to see Colossians as one of God's fullest explanations of how Christians are to live the Christian life. The clarity of the theme has so focused my heart upon the person and work of Jesus Christ that it has safeguarded me from many of the false substitutes in our day that sound so good and look so right.

This is by no means an exhaustive study. A verse-by-verse exposition would have been ten times the length of this book! Rather, this is a discovery of how Jesus Christ is uniquely unveiled in Colossians as a whole and how we are radically transformed by that revelation. This is simply a flyover of these pages to give you the spirit of the book. Once you understand the big picture, all the individual verses all come together. By seeing the guiding principle behind why this letter was written, may the reader enter into an increasing knowledge of God and experience continual transformation into the image of the Son of God by faith.

The How of Holiness

Although God's holiness permeates every one of the 66 books of our Bible, Colossians offers perhaps the fullest explanation of the *how* of holiness, of how to live a life well-pleasing to the Lord. Yes, God wants me to be holy, but *how* do I do that? In Colossians God answers that big how for us. Though Colossians is filled with complex thoughts about Jesus Christ, these are all clustered around a single, simple theme. The simple message of Colossians is for every Christian to possess Christ here and now, not just in future glory when we go to heaven.

Colossians is neatly divided into two halves. The first two chapters expound upon the doctrines of the Savior and His redemptive activities. It is a "gospel concentrate" of what God has done for each believer in the Lord Jesus Christ. The last two chapters develop the practical outworkings of receiving such an awesome Savior.

I believe the key verse that encapsulates God's intent for the whole letter is this:

> Therefore as you have received Christ Jesus the Lord, so walk in Him (Colossians 2:6).

This simplified summary serves as a general rule of thumb. Although the big theme of each chapter of Colossians overlaps the others, each chapter does have its own unique predominating theme. The predominant theme of chapter 1 is Christ Himself, as spotlighted by our key verse: "as you have received *Christ*." Along with John 1 and Hebrews 1, this chapter is notably one of the most Christ-centered (Christological, in the parlance of the theologian) in the Bible. This chapter is saturated with exalted portraits of the preeminent Lord Jesus Christ as Creator, Redeemer, Reconciler, Head of the Church, and other glories.

Chapter 2 is about our reception or appropriation of Christ: "as you have *received* Christ, so walk in Him." It speaks about receiving Christ as an unearned, undeserved gift. In Jesus we have already received the fullness of the Godhead bodily, circumcision, resurrection, forgiveness, among other blessings. It also says what receiving Christ is not. We received Christ, the body or substance, not shadows of Old Testament preparatory pictures, supposed visions of angels, or commandments of men.

Chapters 3 and 4 emphasize the practical life of faith: "as you have received Christ, *so walk in Him.*" Chapter 3 depicts the outworkings of Christ received. So Paul heads the list with victory over the sins of the flesh, followed by the putting on Christ in godly character. The rest of chapter 3 shows what human relationships look like when we've received Christ: husbands and wives, fathers and children, masters and slaves. Chapter 4 underscores the same outworkings of receiving Christ, this time illustrating it using real-life people.

These last two chapters give us a sample, not an exhaustive list. These examples serve to identify the underlying principle so that we can apply it to every area of our Christian life. Colossians blessedly announces the *how* of experiencing every other list in the Bible—the fruit of the Spirit, the gifts of the Spirit, the character lists in the pastoral epistles, the life of Christ shown us in the four Gospels.

Colossians 3:1-4 is another passage that shows how believing the gospel, the word of God that presents our Lord Jesus, transitions to living it out. These are the pivotal "*As...so*" of "as you have received Christ, so walk in Him." Failure to grasp how to turn the corner from faith in Christ to experiencing the truth according to godliness results in many unhappy and frustrating experiences—legalism, barrenness, joylessness, discouragement, hopelessness, and corruption of thought, word, and deed. This Spirit-inspired, Christ-saturated transition is intended to lift us to the heights of faith for which every earnest child of God yearns—to see Christ glorified in our body, whether by life or by death. God has so designed this epistle to breathe fresh life into our sanctification—our actual conformity to Christ in thought, word, and deed. A right understanding of the purpose of God is a rudder that steers our course into a sanctified life.

A Transforming Vision of God Transforms

A great temptation is to think of God as a doting grandfather just sporadically handing out grace to His grandkids. Or perhaps we think of God after the manner of a soup kitchen volunteer ladling out just enough grace in the bowl to get the down-and-outers through the day. Our head tells us that God is fabulously wealthy beyond imagination, but our experience says He just gives us periodic sprinkles of Christ, eking out only enough to ride out the storms of life. Sin still seems a raging tyrant to us. It is a far cry from the daily showers of the Lord that fulfill His gospel promise to bless us and make us a blessing to all the families of the earth (Genesis 12:1-3). It is an experience that knows not the Lord's promise of *rivers*—not trickles nor even river (singular)—of living waters flowing out (John 7:37-39).

It is my hope that a careful observation of these passages in their context will transform your vision of God as an abundant giver of Jesus Christ for every situation, for every relationship, for every ministry, at all times, and all places. The good news is that the source of all these riches is the Lord Jesus Christ, whose blood has reconciled us to God. May God open up our understanding how to apply the gospel declarations of the first half of the book towards godly practice in daily life! A right understanding of the heart of God will motivate you to pray, like Paul, for yourself and others to be filled with the knowledge of His will, namely, God delights and rejoices to clothe us daily with Christ. We are familiar with the prodigal's father whose joy could not withhold the best robe. Our Father in heaven is as joyful or more to clothe us in His best Robe—His beloved Son, our Lord Jesus Christ, the One who loves us and gave Himself for us!

CHAPTER 2
Christ Preeminent

Colossal themes of Jesus Christ's person and work anchor our hope in Him as our one-stop-shop for holiness in the cruddy here and now. It doesn't take long in reading Colossians to be struck with the preeminence of Christ. Now, Paul didn't magnify Jesus Christ so there'd be great material for the Christology chapter in theology books twenty centuries later. No, Paul was writing to real people with real problems. God's wise solution for the real problems of this life is the preeminence of Christ.

Preeminence as it's commonly used refers to a dominant or prominent rank in a comparative list. For example, the United States today is preeminent in its military expenditures, spending more than the next eight largest nations of the world combined. As Paul applies preeminence in Colossians, Christ is *infinitely more* preeminent than anything else in the universe. To try to get our heads around this humongous difference, take water as an example of a prominent substance of Earth, covering three-fourths of its surface. Infinitesimal, ubiquitous atoms would be preeminent, being the universal building block of water along with every other substance of our world. So atoms are infinitely preeminent in the sense that they eclipse even oceans of water. Jesus' preeminence, like that of atoms, is everywhere present though not observable. However, every analogy breaks down at some point, as atoms are innumerable whereas Jesus is one. But that transcendence above everything else better conveys the superlative, qualitative difference between Colossians' use of preeminence and today's vernacular (i.e., the largest in a list of comparable items). His preeminence is far greater than the farthest reaches of our minds to imagine! I desire to draw your attention to what Scripture says it means to have Christ preeminent in your life.

Paul, in writing this letter, is not advocating for Jesus to be preeminent as first in the list of many. In American history, George Washington and Abraham Lincoln stand out prominently among the many presidents. We even have a day dedicated to them in February called President's Day. Great feats at critical junctures of our nation's history catapulted them to a conspicuous place of honor and dignity. Now, Jesus Christ is the King of kings—and presidents. He is infinitely preeminent over all the U.S. presidents, for He that created these great men—Washington and Lincoln—is greater than they, just as the architect is greater than the house he built (Hebrews 3:3). Not only is He preeminent over them but over *every* great world ruler from the Pharaohs and Caesars down to the present day. So Jesus Christ is not merely at the top of the list among many, like Washington and Lincoln, but boundlessly preeminent—above all.

Many put Jesus first on the list of life's priorities,

followed by family and friends, work and church, and other passions like fishing or bingo or video games. That would be more like prominence. Preeminence, as it's applied to Jesus, means that He transcends all our lists. This is not just playing with words; it signifies a totally different direction of the heart and life. A failure in heart trust in Christ as immeasurably preeminent is missing out on the abundant life of Christ pervading all of life's lists.

If you're like me, you have a tendency to compartmentalize your life. We have "church life" roped off on Sunday mornings, over "family life" sectioned off there, "work life" from 8 to 5 Monday through Friday, and whatever other little boxes that define our existence. In this mode of thinking, Jesus can be very prominent in our lives. We have a "quiet time" in the morning where we put Jesus first. Then we go about our daily agendas, giving hardly a thought about our heavenly identity in the Lord Jesus. Perhaps we have other little boxes in our day devoted to Jesus—singing in the car, reading the Bible during a lunch break, memorizing a Scripture verse after dinner, praying before bedtime. Though Jesus may be first place in our list of priorities, that does not mean we've grasped the message of Colossians where He is preeminent. Jesus being prominent—first in a list of everything—is not what God is after in the book of Colossians. If Jesus is first, that naturally implies something is second. When Jesus is preeminent, there is no second or third or fourth; Christ is all.

Joseph Parker, a British Presbyterian writer in the nineteenth century, encapsulated the heart and soul of the surpassing preeminence of Jesus Christ using this vivid imagery:

> Jesus Christ was *not a figure on a landscape*: he was and is the life of all living things....in the case of Jesus Christ I

want nothing but Christ: I want the landscape to fade away into an invisible fleck, and nothing to be seen but the CHRIST, filling all things and making all things look small under his infinite presence.[5]

So what exactly does it mean for Jesus to be *preeminent* in my life? If you are scratching your head about what this means, you are not alone. I have often wrestled with trying to understand this. As we embark on our journey together through Colossians, we'll try to answer that question. Ask your Father God to teach you by His Spirit in Colossians what it means practically for Jesus to be preeminent in your life.

Christ Preeminent: Firstborn of All Creation

We are considering the first mega theme—preeminence. In chapters 1 and 2, Paul pulls the divine scrapbook off the shelf and shows us these amazing snapshots of what God has already done for us in Christ. He simply desires for us to sit back in our easy chair and relish each snapshot of the grandeur and excellencies of the Lord Jesus. With the whole universe in his panoramic lens, Paul draws our attention to how Jesus Christ is preeminent both in creation and in the new creation, the church.

> He is the image of the invisible God, the firstborn of all creation. For by him all things were created, in heaven and on earth, visible and invisible, whether thrones or dominions or rulers or authorities—all things were created through him and for him. And he is before all

---

[5] Joseph Parker, *These Sayings of Mine*, (New York: I. K. Funk & Co., Publishers, 1881), p. 2

things, and in him all things hold together. And he is the head of the body, the church. He is the beginning, the firstborn from the dead, that in everything he might be preeminent (Colossians 1:15-18 ESV).

Firstborn in *the firstborn of all creation* does not mean, as some argue, that Jesus Christ was the first creation in a line of created beings. Our Lord Jesus is totally one with God the Father (John 10:30). Christ's title as "the Alpha and Omega" (Revelation 22:13) lays claim to exclusive identity as God with no predecessors, as alpha, being the first letter of the Greek alphabet, has nothing before it. Had the Father created Him, the Son could only truthfully claim to be the "Beta and Omega" but never Alpha and Omega.

Firstborn, therefore, has nothing to do with time of origin but rather rank of importance. The Messiah in the Psalms is said to have been the firstborn among the kings. "I also shall make him My firstborn, the highest of the kings of the earth" (Psalm 89:27). The plain understanding of firstborn is of rank. This Messiah, this Christ, as firstborn is "the highest of the kings of the earth," or as other Bible accolades ascribe, "King of kings and Lord of lords."

The patriarch Jacob, when pronouncing a final blessing on his sons before his death, had these significant words to his firstborn son, Reuben:

Reuben, you are my firstborn, my might, and the firstfruits of my strength, preeminent in dignity and preeminent in power (Genesis 49:3 ESV).

Firstborn clearly points towards preeminence in dignity and power. That which was merely a foreshadowing in Reuben finds all preeminence in dignity and power marvelously fulfilled in Jesus! The Lord Jesus Christ, by whom "all things were created," deserves exalted honor as "the firstborn of all creation," as Hebrews attests:

> For Jesus has been counted worthy of more glory than Moses—as much more glory as the builder of a house has more honor than the house itself. (For every house is built by someone, but the builder of all things is God.) (Hebrews 3:3-4 ESV)

Rembrandt is more honored than his paintings, Michelangelo than his sculptures, Thomas Edison than his inventions, Frank Lloyd Wright than his buildings, and Albert Einstein than his theories. How much more honor does God, who created Rembrandt, Michelangelo, Edison, Wright, and Einstein, get! Jesus Christ as "the builder of all things" and "firstborn of all creation" deserves the preeminent place, worthy of the highest recognition and glory!

Christ Preeminent: Firstborn from the Dead

Having observed Christ's preeminence in creation, let's now look to the crux of Christ's preeminence in the church:

> And he is the head of the body, the church. He is the beginning, the firstborn from the dead, that in everything he might be preeminent (Colossians 1:18 ESV).

Firstborn is repeated in a slightly different context. Jesus is *the firstborn from the dead*. Again, the reference to firstborn does not signify time of origin. Hundreds of years before Jesus, the prophets Elijah and Elisha had been instruments in raising the dead. So *firstborn from the dead* means highest in rank of importance, because all saints from the beginning of time to the end are absolutely, utterly dependent upon His resurrection! Romans 6 heralds the good news that our walking in newness of life is due to the preeminence that Christ's resurrection has among all believers.

> Or do you not know that all of us who have been baptized into Christ Jesus have been baptized into His death? Therefore we have been buried with Him through baptism into death, so that as Christ was raised from the dead through the glory of the Father, so we too might walk in newness of life (Romans 6:3-4).

The death of Jesus stands out dramatically from all other events in human history. This is because Jesus is our substitute who suffered the full penalty of God's wrath that our sins deserved. He graciously paid the debt we could never repay by His broken body and shed blood. Because He died for our sins, we need not. Jesus paid it all; all to Him I owe.

The glorious truth of substitution is applied in Romans 6 to Christ's death and burial. Every Christian has been baptized, that is, fully immersed or submerged, in Christ Jesus. Our inclusion into Christ 2,000 years ago means being included into every aspect of His finished work. So when Jesus Christ died to sin, because we've been included in Him, we are dead to sin. Sin no longer has power over us because it no longer has power over Christ! Because Christ was buried, we were buried in Him. The good news of this connection is that when Christ was raised from the tomb, we were too!

This is the glorious truth of Jesus as my substitute. I cannot fly; planes can fly. When I am in the airplane, I fly. *I* cannot die to sin nor walk in the newness of life. *Christ* is dead to sin and does walk in the newness of life. When I am *in Christ* my substitute, I am dead to sin and alive to God, walking in the newness of life.[6] This is the glorious news of Jesus as the firstborn from the dead, that in everything He might be preeminent. Jesus as the firstborn from the dead illustrates what all the people of God who are united to Him can expect. All the benefits and privileges bestowed upon Christ as the firstborn are likewise showered upon all His brothers.

The Golden Chain of Christ's Preeminence in Everything

Jesus is the firstborn from the dead. Christ has the highest rank of the resurrection; His is the resurrection of all resurrections.

> He is the beginning, the firstborn from the dead, that in everything he might be preeminent.

The little word *that* is the crucial link in the golden chain of Christ's preeminence in everything. Let's not miss what it is that makes Jesus Christ preeminent in the new creation: "He is...the firstborn from the dead, *that* in everything he might be preeminent."[7] The reason for Jesus Christ becoming in all things the One who is preeminent is due to His being the firstborn from the dead, the highest in rank of all the resurrected dead. *In everything* refers in

---

[6] I am indebted to Ed Miller bringing this airplane analogy to bear on our substitution in Christ

[7] *That* in the Greek is *hina* (HEE-nah), a very common conjunction that denotes purpose or result (i.e., in order that). Kenneth Wuest's New Testament translation employs as many English words as needed to convey the original sense of the Greek text. I find Wuest's translation of this verse especially enlightening: "...in order that [*hina*] He might become in all things Himself the one who is preeminent."

context to the church. *The resurrection of Jesus from the dead is the golden link that joins His preeminence with everything in the church.* For Jesus to be continuously preeminent in His people was dependent upon Him being the firstborn from the dead.

In the natural creation, the Lord is preeminent in that He holds all things together. He feeds all living creatures and provides for their every need—light, air, food, water, warmth. The basic elements of this earthly sphere serve as shadows and preparations for the spiritual, eternal things. In the new creation, because Christ died and rose again, He supplies every need for all its blood-bought citizens. Our bread of faith is Christ's broken body. Our drink is now a trusting in Christ's blood that has blotted out all of our sins. Our water is the Holy Spirit of God, welling up within us as a spring of life, flowing out as rivers. Our light is Christ, the true Light that enlightens every man. Jesus' death and resurrection was essential for God's eternal goal of making Jesus preeminent in all things pertaining to the church. Since this is God's goal, are we coming more into conformity with His purpose?

CHAPTER 3
The Real Problem

Jesus Christ is enormous, gigantic, titanic—immeasurably surpassing every need of the entire universe! Paul's opening curtain unveils the preeminence of Jesus Christ to generate hope. Hope in Jesus Christ answers the real problem facing these Colossian believers, and by extension, every believer in every age.

Much has been said by commentators and preachers about the false teachings in Colossae. They were a problem, but not the primary problem. Everything we need to understand the main point is contained within the epistle itself. We don't need to strain at extra-biblical sources to figure out the exact recipe that made up these errant teachings. Paul simply gave us a sampling of representative ingredients. The Judaizers had their hand in the pie, advocating Old Testament ceremonial laws like Sabbaths and festivals. The Gnostics were cooking up unbiblical notions that spiritual things are good and material things are evil. So the focus of Paul's letter is not an exhaustive treatise on false teachings. What is essential is that we grasp the *principle* animating them. Professor Paul desires that we graduate from the elementary teachings to our doctorate in Christ Jesus in order to lead us from problem to solution.

Christians today may think they're not duped like the Colossians because they don't practice the list of chapter 2. "I don't get into all the Jewish dietary laws. I can eat pork and shrimp. I am not in bondage to keeping the Sabbath and the Passover." Yet because of a failure to understand the underlying principles, that same Christian can be in far greater danger than the Colossians ever were! We can sport a fluent New Testament vocabulary while the quality of our Christian life is not all that much different from a Jew under the Old Testament, filled with meticulous observances of commandments and slavish adherence to external things like priests and temples. So if we see this list as a checklist of dos and don'ts rather than hearing what the Spirit says in principle, we've totally missed the point. If we are ever to be presented mature and complete in Christ, we must be properly warned of the subtle enemies infiltrating our thinking. There is nothing new under the sun. The subtle philosophies then are still alive and kicking now, just repackaged to modern twenty-first century tastes.

In our day, these same philosophies can be dressed up as "Read your Bible every day, have a quiet time, go to church a lot, make sure you have a family worship time, and pray and fast. Have faith! Get a biblical worldview!" Does this surprise you? Is it good for us to read our Bible every day? Of course! Should we pray? Of course! These are lovely byproducts of a life passionately occupied with Jesus Christ. But if we miss the principle that Paul is laboring to show us, we can turn our eyes towards these good fruits and away from Christ the Vine from which all these wonderful evidences of grace grow. Because these philosophies skirt so close to the truth, they are as hidden reefs threatening to capsize our vessel in an apparently safe harbor. Missing the principles dopes our spiritual senses to the real danger. A solid grasp of the principles, on the other hand, puts us on full alert against the alluring and subtle snares in the world, within ourselves and even within Christendom. We can be led astray by the preacher who dazzles us with the biblical meanings of the Greek and Hebrew. The tragic thing is that these thorns left undetected secretly choke out our only hope—Christ in us, the hope of the glory.

Warnings are blessings from God. Warnings serve us by identifying things as they really are and not as they seem. They steer us away from the unfulfilling tares of spiritual-sounding wisdom that we may be satiated with the Wheat, our Lord Jesus Christ, who is the Bread of Life.

A Root of Discouragement

The false teachers were not the real problem facing the believers in Colossae. They were the *occasion* that uncovered the root issue for what it was. What was that root problem?

Unlike other churches Paul wrote to in their day, the Colossians appear at first to be a fairly low maintenance congregation. They were not experiencing intense persecution like the Thessalonians. They were not strutting around like peacocks with their chests puffed out like the Corinthians were over spiritual gifts. They had not fallen over the cliff into legalism like the foolish Galatians. Yet the problem in Colossae so alarmed the aged apostle that he agonized in prayer over it and felt impelled to pen this four-chapter epistle that we now hold in our hands. What was that problem?

These Colossian saints were doing extremely well in many areas. Paul commends them several times on their faith in Jesus Christ. He says glowingly that he was "rejoicing to see your good order and the firmness of your faith in Christ" (Colossians 2:5 ESV). He also recognized the work of God in their love. Upon his hearing of their love in the Spirit, his heart was stirred to pray for them. "We always thank God...when we pray for you, since we heard of...the love that you have for all the saints" (1:3-4 ESV). They had the crown jewel, love, adorning their daily lives. These believers were also commended for spiritual fruit. They were bringing forth fruit from the day that they heard and believed the gospel (1:6). In many ways, this looked like a vibrant and healthy church. If a visitor came into the Lycus Valley looking for a good church, someone might say, "Oh, you've got to check out the church of Colossae!"

But there was a subtle problem, lurking as a hungry wolf in the shadows, that threatened this passionately devoted flock. Only by the infinite wisdom of the eternal Spirit did the imprisoned apostle put his thumb on the pulse of the problem. A symptom of the trouble was the Colossian believers' misdirected hope. Instead of grounding their hopes securely in the Lord Jesus Christ for the A-to-Z of a God-pleasing life, these faithful brothers were being seduced by these philosophies and "biblical" techniques that sounded so good and so right. So while on the surface it seemed that the big dilemma facing the Colossian church was these erroneous teachers, it was much deeper than that. *The root problem for the Colossians—and for you and me—is discouragement.*

When reading and rereading this short epistle, the root problem being discouragement may not jump out at us.

The windbags spouting off their philosophies and false doctrines may detract us from seeing that. This discouragement is not announced by way of frequent appearance in the letter but rather by the intensity in which it is presented. A close examination of the letter's contents brings discouragement to light by spiritual warfare (2:1-3), by apostolic commission to the letter carrier (4:8), and by the contents of the epistle itself.

Warring for the Discouraged Heart

At the end of chapter 1, Paul wrote, "For this I toil, struggling with all his energy that he powerfully works within me" (Colossians 1:29 ESV). Paul's toiling to preach Christ is spoken of in military terms like a conflict against a formidable foe. The Greek word for *struggling* is *agonizomai* (ah-goh-NEE-zoh-mahy), which means to contend for a prize. This is where we get our English word "agonize." Paul continues to provide more detail about this struggle:

> For I want you to know how great a struggle [*agon*] I have for you and for those at Laodicea and for all who have not seen me face to face, that their hearts may be encouraged (Colossians 2:1-2 ESV).

Thayer's defines *agon* (ah-GOHN), the Greek word for "struggle," as "the place of contest, the arena or stadium." So Paul in a picturesque way ushers the Colossian believers to their seats in a great coliseum as spectators of his wrestling in prayer according to the divine energy of Christ at work in him. Paul wrote in Ephesians, the sister epistle to Colossians, that we wrestle not with flesh and blood but against the spiritual principalities and powers, those angelic antagonists aligned with Satan against the children of God. Paul wanted these Colossian believers to know about this wrestling in intercession on their behalf while he was detained in a Roman prison.

What was this valiant contest over? The prize is clearly stated: "that their *hearts may be encouraged.*" The word for *that* is the common conjunction *hina* (HEE-nah), which we referred to earlier as denoting purpose, *in order that.* Paul's agonizing in prayer for these Colossian saints had this purpose in view: encouragement! If Paul prayed for them to be *encouraged,* the obvious implication is that they were *discouraged.* So we too are invited to witness this gladiatorial-like contest over a peculiar prize— encouragement.

Commissioned to Encourage

Not only does this intense spiritual wrestling match over discouragement clue us into the real issue with the Colossians, but Paul mentions another significant one. Somebody had to deliver the letter from the Roman prison the many treacherous miles over land and sea back to Colossae. What was Paul's chief charge to the mail carrier? Encouragement!

> Tychicus will tell you all about my activities. He is a beloved brother and faithful minister and fellow servant in the Lord. *I have sent him to you for this very purpose,* that you may know how we are and *that he may encourage your hearts* (Colossians 4:7-8 ESV).

Paul expressly states why he sent Tychicus to them. The first reason was to let everybody know how he was doing in Rome. The second reason, more importantly, was "that he may encourage your hearts." Paul laid his intercessory burden upon the trusted shoulders of beloved, faithful Tychicus. Now Tychicus was not just an ordinary mailman, but a close, trusted coworker of the apostle. In Acts 20:4 Tychicus was chosen by the churches as a trustworthy courier to accompany Paul to Jerusalem with the gifts from the Gentile churches. He was a qualified ministry gift that Paul trusted to relieve Titus on the island of Crete (Titus 3:12). What is implied in the Titus epistle is that Tychicus had proven fruit in the characteristics of an overseer—above reproach, hospitable, a lover of good, self-controlled, upright, holy, and disciplined. The principles of a well-ordered life were at work in brother Tychicus.

Paul's ministerial picks were of a high spiritual caliber, like Timothy, whom he contrasted with many Christian workers who "all seek after their own interests, not those of Christ Jesus" (Philippians 2:21). As Paul's life drew to a close, Tychicus was still faithfully acting on Paul's behalf, this time providing relief in Ephesus so that Timothy could come quickly to minister to him in Rome (2 Timothy 4:12-13). Paul could discharge the burden of his heart— encouraging a discouraged group of brothers in Colossae— to Tychicus, "our beloved brother and faithful servant and fellow bond-servant in the Lord" (Colossians 4:7).

So not only did Paul agonize in intercession for their encouragement, but he sent a trusted ministry gift to do the same. The apostle administered a gift of consolation, Tychicus, to encourage these discouraged saints. Here is a second strong indicator that Paul's thumb was on the pulse of discouragement in the Colossian church.

The Table of Contents: Encouragement
A final indication that discouragement was the root issue

facing the Colossian saints is in the contents of the letter itself. The whole epistle is an antidote to discouragement. Paul in big broad strokes paints a colossal Christ who is the centerpiece of creation and the new creation. This galactic, cosmic Christ they'd received at the beginning is the same Christ to remedy their discouragement.

So the main problem in Colossae was not the observable issue of the false teachers. These were the weeds at the surface. The soil which allowed these weeds to take root was the discouragement of the Colossian Christians. It was this discouragement that opened the door for these false teachers to gain a foothold in their hearts. Their waning confidence in Christ's preeminence made these false teachings so enticing. So what was it that were they discouraged about?

Why So Downcast O My Soul?

The cause of the discouragement can be deduced from the empty promises the false teachers were holding out. Through chapter 2 Paul builds his case against the false teachers by contrasting their wisdom with Christ, "in whom are hidden all the treasures of wisdom and knowledge." After demonstrating the deficiencies of their wisdom, his closing summary directly addresses his opponents:

> These have indeed an appearance of wisdom in promoting self-made religion and asceticism and severity to the body, but they are of no value in stopping the indulgence of the flesh (Colossians 2:23 ESV).

At the crux of this wisdom was an appeal to holiness: stopping the indulgence of the flesh. That's what made these messages so appealing. These lovers of the Lord Jesus were perplexed over what to do about their flesh. They wanted to live a holy life, but were beset by the recurring sin patterns in their lives. Paul addresses some of these problems among the Colossians: "But now you must put them all away: anger, wrath, malice, slander, and obscene talk from your mouth" (Colossians 3:8 ESV).

Because of their desire to please the Lord with a holy life, their relapse into old sins opened up temptation to look outside Jesus for help. Somehow they thought that Christ Jesus the Lord that they'd received through hearing the gospel was good enough to get them into the kingdom, but to live consistent, holy lives, they needed something more. Their faith was being shaken and they were losing hope in the objective, unchanging truth of the gospel: Jesus Christ alone is more than enough. To add to Jesus is to nullify Him. This is what alarmed God's apostle. It should alarm us, too.

CHAPTER 4

Christ is the Beginning

In my elementary school days, I vividly remember my first wonderment with seeds. Autumn pumpkin carving led to a new discovery of the orange pulpy innards full of large seeds. Curiosity took hold of me to plant some seeds in a paper towel, soaked with water, in a clear plastic cup so I could watch what happened. I was fascinated by the quick growth, as roots and stalk progressively emerged from the once hard shell, now swollen and soft, reaching skyward with new green leaves and fuzzy stem.

Paul draws from nature to teach spiritual lessons. "For since the creation of the world His invisible attributes, His eternal power and divine nature, have been clearly seen" (Romans 1:20). So created things are excellent teaching tools to take us forward into the knowledge of Christ, who is the exact image of the invisible God (Hebrews 1:3). God's divine nature and invisible attributes are clearly seen in the whole earth that is full of His glory, not the least of which includes the tiny seed.

The Gospel Seed

Paul makes skillful use of agricultural metaphors in the book of Colossians, particularly in accord with the Genesis vignette of "fruit trees on the earth bearing fruit after their kind with seed in them." In Colossians he likens the word of truth, the gospel, to a seed that has matured to constantly and increasingly bear fruit.

> The word of truth, the gospel...has come to you, just as in all the world also *it is constantly bearing fruit and increasing*, even as it has been doing in you also since the day you heard of it and understood the grace of God in truth; just as you learned it from Epaphras, our beloved fellow bond-servant (Colossians 1:5-7).

The apostle Peter also likened the Bible, the written word of God, to a seed. He says that "you have been born again not of seed which is perishable but imperishable, that is, through the living and enduring word of God" (1 Peter 1:23). Similarly, Jesus' famous parable of the sower compares the word of God to a seed which grows with varying results in the hearts of the hearers. Epaphras was the sower among the Colossian believers, for it was through him that they learned the gospel. So their hearts were the fertile soil from which the word of truth took root, grew, bore fruit, and continually increased. As a seed abides in soil, so God's word needs a soil, that is, our hearts.

A seed appears to be lifeless, yet there is a mystery of dormant life resident within. Some seeds have been known to survive as long as 150 years and still produce life. Like Sleeping Beauty awaiting the kiss of a prince, the seed contains the potential for life awaiting the right conditions to awaken. The Holy Spirit is the living water that awakens the dormant life of the seed of God's word within the heart.

Our 14-foot blue spruce, kitty-corner to our front porch, is host to two bird feeders that my two boys nailed and glued together for one of their monthly Home Depot crafts. It fascinates me to watch the birds that frequent them—sparrows, chickadees, a rare red cardinal. To stock my sons' carpentry masterpieces, I bought a 20-pound bag of bird seed from Home Depot (well, I guess those free kids workshops are pretty smart for business after all!). With all those seeds tightly packed together, that bag is very hard and rigid. There is a spiritual lesson for us here.

Reading or memorization of Scripture can be like that 20-pound bag of bird seeds, all packed in there but hard and stiff. Christians who have the shell of the word of God without Christ the resident life can be like that—hard and stiff, critical, judgmental, difficult to be around.

So what we need is not the seed alone, but the Spirit who manifests Christ out of the word into our daily lives. Jesus Christ is the living Word, the true life, divinely designed to emerge from the spoken or written word of truth. Jesus noted this distinction while addressing the Bible experts of His day:

> You search the Scriptures because you think that in them you have eternal life; it is these that testify about Me; and you are unwilling to come to Me so that you may have life (John 5:39-40).

Earlier on in my Christian life I believed that the Bible was like food for my spirit, so if I "ate" a lot of it (i.e., read the Scriptures a lot), I would have eternal life—my life could shine with the glory of God akin to the glow on Moses' face. But in hindsight I see now that approach is like giving a destitute starving man a can of beans without a can opener. The nutritious life is in there, but it must be opened to benefit from it. Likewise Christ is the life "locked up" in Scripture, for we must come to Him to have eternal life. We must approach God's word in the way it was intended to bring us to Christ.

We need to apply God's divine "can opener" so we can satisfy our desperate hunger and be filled. God freely gives the Spirit to reveal our Lord Jesus Christ, the living Word, from the written word that testifies of Him. The Spirit is available simply by asking. "If you then, being evil, know how to give good gifts to your children, how much more will your heavenly Father give the Holy Spirit to those who ask Him?" (Luke 11:13) I have made it a regular habit to ask God to fill me with the Holy Spirit before I read the Scripture. This has been easy because I am aware of how destitute and needy I am without His help. Priceless have been the eye-opening adventures of having Christ revealed from God's word.

Christ the Living Word

Seeds are the beginning of new life. Every plant starts with a seed. To this discouraged Colossian band of brothers Paul stresses going back to the beginning. That's why the letter opens with much attention fixed upon the seed—the word of truth, the gospel. From day one we received the word of God as a very fruitful seed yielding a Person—Jesus Christ, the Beginning. From the beginning of creation, God has highlighted the vital role that seeds have.

> Then God said, "Let the earth sprout vegetation, plants yielding seed, and fruit trees on the earth bearing fruit after their kind with seed in them"; and it was so. The earth brought forth vegetation, plants yielding seed after their kind, and trees bearing fruit with seed in them, after

their kind; and God saw that it was good (Genesis 1:11-12).

If you plant a peach seed, you'll get peaches. If you plant an apple seed, you'll get apples. Just as nature teaches us that each seed produces after its own kind, Paul stresses that we hold fast and are not moved away from what we heard in the beginning. When the Colossians learned the gospel message from Epaphras, they received the words as seeds that yield after their kind. Paul pinpoints the beginning of transformation in the Colossians' lives to the day they first "heard in the word of truth" (Colossians 1:5). He also advises, "As you have received Christ Jesus the Lord, so walk in Him" (2:6). So they received much more than words; they received Christ Himself, the dormant life resident within those words. That's why we're admonished to remain true to that gospel seed that yields the lovely Tree of Life—Christ—blooming and blossoming in the new Eden creation in our hearts. As the divine wisdom unfolds through the epistle, we will come to see that what was "constantly bearing fruit and increasing" was the Lord Jesus Himself!

When we receive the word of God through proclamation, the Spirit overshadows the seed of the preached word to manifest the living Word, Christ. So it could also be said, "as you have received Christ," for so they did. The Spirit and the word worked together to germinate the unsearchable riches of Christ Jesus the Lord in their hearts. When Paul relayed how Epaphras "informed us of your love in the Spirit," he recognized that their love that commenced with hearing the word developed in cooperation with the Holy Spirit (Colossians 1:8).

When Mary received the word of God from the angel Gabriel, the Spirit overshadowed her and germinated that seed into the Son of God. The same Spirit seeks to do that again and again, not as a physical baby in a womb, but bringing forth the Son of God in our hearts, the true temple that God erects and not man. "My little children," Paul urged the Galatians, "for whom I am again in the anguish of childbirth until Christ is formed in you!" (Galatians 4:19 ESV).

Jesus is the Beginning

The beginning is not so much a point of time (though from our frame of reference it is) as it is a person, Jesus Christ!

> [Christ] is also head of the body, the church; and *He is the beginning*, the firstborn from the dead, so that He Himself will come to have first place in everything (Colossians 1:18).

Jesus once asked His disciples, "Who do men say that I am?" Today if we ask that question, we'd often hear "Shepherd" or "Lord" or "Savior" or "King" or a number of other common titles of His. But I can't think of a time when someone has ever said, "Jesus is the Beginning." Yet Paul boldly states, "He is the beginning." Jesus, in Revelation, echoes the same, calling Himself "the Beginning of the creation of God" (Revelation 3:14). Of Christ as the Beginning, Charles J. Rolls eloquently observes:

> Christ Himself is the Originator of the mighty powers and processes that produced the present order of things; He is the Overseer of all forms and fashions of life, and the objective toward which all things tend and in which they terminate....In the astronomical realm Christ is said to be the Star and Sun; in the animal kingdom He is declared to be the Lion of Judah and the Lamb of God; in the

biological world He is titled the Tree of Life and Fount. of Life...and in the philological field He is Alpha and Omega and the Word. Investigate where we will, not a grain of grace, not a mite of mercy, not a spark of sympathy, not an atom of authority, not a trace of truth, not a fraction of faith, not a look of love and not a glow of glory exist without His originating energy.[8]

To stay safe in a dangerous world trying to shake and shift off our hope of the gospel we had at first, we'd better understand what Jesus as the Beginning really means. For it is a key to avoiding susceptibility to false paths (many so-called "Christian") and clinging to the true—knowing the will of God that leads us to fruitfulness in every good work.

"He is the beginning" points to Christ becoming the one who is preeminent in our salvation experience. From God's point of view, the beginning of our salvation is not merely about Christ, as a plan of salvation, a Romans road, or four spiritual laws, but is Christ Himself. "As you have received Christ Jesus the Lord," Paul writes, "so walk in Him" (Colossians 2:6). Our salvation begins with receiving Christ. Our starting point did not begin by receiving a philosophy, a religion, a church affiliation, or a list of dos and don'ts. We received a person—Jesus, the Beginning, "the Originator of the mighty powers and processes that produced the present order" of our spiritual lives.

The fallen world in which we live inhales narcissistic, me-centered air incessantly, and it affects the way we view salvation. While we talk in terms of making Jesus our personal Savior, God sees salvation centered in Jesus, who personally adopts us into His massive family as sons and

---

[8] Rolls, Charles J, *The Indescribable Christ: Names and Titles of Jesus Christ A - G* (Neptune, New Jersey: Loizeaux Brothers, 1983), pp. 38-39

daughters. Colossians gives salvation from *God's* point of view: it is *Christ* who is the beginning! Christ is the central figure, the hero, of our story, not us.

Conquering the Scum of All Our Nature

Isabelle Kuhn, a missionary in the earlier part of the twentieth century, received this counsel from a returning missionary: "When you get to China, all the scum of your nature will rise to the top."[9] Now you don't have to be a missionary to encounter this. All of life's difficulties have the unsettling result of dredging up all the scum of our nature to the top. Consider, though, that hardships do not produce the grumbling, discontentment, anger, fear, or variety of fleshly responses. If one bumps a full glass of salty water, the sudden jarring movement didn't produce the salt; it merely revealed what was already in there.

The Colossian believers, while attempting to live lives pleasing to the Lord were experiencing the scum of all their nature rising to the top. So to conquer that filth they turned aside from the gospel to the "touch not" and ascetic practices of the false teachers, to Paul's great consternation. It is absolutely vital that we see Christ as our beginning. The cleaning up of the scum from the very first was not due to our self effort, strict attention to spiritual disciplines, or zealous performance. No, as we first received by faith this colossal, preeminent Christ who is the head of all rule and authority, *God* cleaned up the scum.

Christ was made to be our peace with God. He is our beginning as our reconciler to eradicate the grime of our evil

---

[9] Benge, Janet & Geoff, *Isobel Kuhn: On the Roof of the World* (Seattle, WA: YWAM Publishing, 2010), p. 82

thoughts and deeds.

> For it was the Father's good pleasure for all the fullness to dwell in Him, *and through Him to reconcile all things to Himself,* having made peace through the blood of His cross; through Him, I say, whether things on earth or things in heaven. And although you were formerly alienated and hostile in mind, engaged in evil deeds, *yet He has now reconciled you in His fleshly body through death,* in order to present you before Him holy and blameless and beyond reproach (Colossians 1:19-22).

We all know what reconciliation means. If we've ever gotten into a dispute with a loved one or friend and experienced an awkward relational distance, then we "kissed and made up" to experience the closeness again. That's reconciliation on a human level. Paul here says that "although you were formerly alienated" from God, you are now reconciled. The restoration of this friendship was accomplished "in His fleshly body through death," speaking of Jesus' death on the cross. Our resurrected Champion has purged our scum of being "hostile in mind" to having the stainless "mind of Christ" (1 Corinthians 2:16). The One who sanctifies us has exchanged our willing participation "in doing evil deeds" to "purify for Himself a people for His own possession, zealous for good deeds" (Titus 2:14). The alienation, separation, and awkwardness we had towards God has been put away!

This lovely verse speaks of a reconciliation in this way: "in order to present you before Him holy and blameless and beyond reproach." Jesus alive from the grave acts as firstborn from the dead to present before God the Father all the sons in Himself with all His perfections. Like Mephibosheth, the lame son of King David's friend

Jonathan, we sit as friends at the royal table (2 Samuel 9). "Once Your enemies / now seated at Your table / Jesus, thank You." Christ is made our friend! All these beautiful friendship benefits we experienced at the beginning when we received Christ as our beginning.

As Jesus is the beginning of the created universe, so is He our beginning. All we experienced—peace, reconciliation, cleansing, forgiveness—was all an expression of receiving a person—Christ. Paul reminds a shaken, discouraged group of believers of their introductory experience of scum removal and good fruit production through hearing the good news from brother Epaphras. The good fruit, the fruit of the Spirit, materialized through the emergence of the preeminence of Jesus Christ from the seed of God's word. So God's wisdom admonishes us to hold fast to Christ as our Beginning. We received Christ Jesus the Lord through the preached word of God at the beginning; all our continuing in the fruit of Spirit is no different. "As you have received Christ, so walk in Him."

CHAPTER 5

The Hope of Glory

Hope bridges the gap between discouragement, the root cause of the problem facing the Colossian church, and this preeminent Lord Jesus Christ, who is the Beginning. Having our hope anchored in something other than Jesus leads to devastating consequences. Paul labors painstakingly to ensure that our hope at the beginning remains thoroughly grounded in the Lord Jesus Christ and His finished work, for this gives all the encouragement needed to glorify and please God in this life.

The specific word "hope" is referred to three times in this epistle. Pastor and theologian John Piper lays some groundwork on the meaning of hope:

> Biblical hope is not finger-crossing. It is a confident expectation of good things to come. Hebrews calls it the

"full assurance of hope" (6:11).[10]

So hope is not wishful thinking, knocking on wood, or other superstitious gestures. Daydreaming of winning the lottery is not an expression of biblical hope. In Colossians Paul strategically uses hope as an immovable bedrock of confident expectation in God's promises of the good things to come—good works in us, such as "compassionate hearts, kindness, humility, meekness, and patience" (Colossians 3:12 ESV).

The antidote to discouragement is hope, especially a hope in the *present power* of the gospel's focal point: Christ. Doctor Paul effectively prescribes this medication to cure discouragement and alleviate the symptoms of sin. The active ingredient is the Lord Jesus Christ Himself. When we see what a preeminent Christ we have and are persuaded that this colossal Christ is committed to glory both here and in eternity, hope soars on eagles' wings. This hope best positions our expectant hearts to receive the maximum benefit and timely help from our Great Physician, Jesus Christ.

Hope is the means for remedying all ills of the flesh. Our hope in the present power of Christ answers our inward pining for freedom from the sin that holds us in bondage and depresses us. This hope trusts the Promiser for every God-pleasing fruit of righteousness right here and now, as well as the life to come. Got marital strife? Are the kids driving you crazy? Do other relationship conflicts get you down? Hope in Jesus. Are you bombarded all around with

---

[10] John Piper, "Our Hope: The Appearing of Jesus Christ" (retrieved from http://www.desiringgod.org/resource-library/sermons/our-hope-the-appearing-of-jesus-christ on January 27, 2011)

temptations to sin? Hope in Jesus. Your only hope, Christian, is faith in who Christ is and what He has done and will do for you.

At the bottom of much preaching in our day is the unspoken message of "Do more! Try harder!" Strangely absent is the hope of the gospel's super-eminent Christ for putting to death what is earthly in you and putting on the new self. Much preaching today is not Christ-centered; it is sin-centered, motivating obedience by a perpetual treadmill of guilt. Early in my Christian life I gravitated to sermons that called attention to my persistent shortcomings at witnessing, praying, giving, serving, and looking for the coming of the Lord. The solution, in a nutshell, was try harder—repent more, pray more, read your Bible more, and get more busy about the kingdom of God. That vicious circle of self-condemnation and diligent self-effort really looked holy for a little while as long as I was focused on the shortcoming, but it didn't transform my heart. The "try harder gospel" totally misses the heartbeat of Paul's address to the discouraged Colossian church.

Tethering Our Hope to the Gospel

Hope is closely linked with possessing or appropriating. Hope precedes possession; hope ceases once the desired object is obtained or the long-awaited goal comes to pass. Like the eager child whose hope is tethered to the expectation of opening gifts on Christmas day, that hope vanishes when the unwrapped gifts are in his hands. Paul wrote to the Roman saints:

> For in this hope we were saved. Now hope that is seen is not hope. For who hopes for what he sees? But if we hope for what we do not see, we wait for it with patience

(Romans 8:24-25 ESV).

The Colossians were hoping to see the life of Jesus expressed in their lives. These believers did not understand, though, that Christ is all-sufficient for a God-pleasing victorious life; Jesus is all we need. They understood the power Jesus once had in their conversion to put away immorality, impurity, passion, evil desires, and other sins (Colossians 3:7). Defective in their comprehension, however, was that this same Jesus whom they'd first received was totally sufficient to continue empowering their spiritual lives. "Yes, Christ worked well for a lot of things, just not everything." Colossians exposes this fatal flaw of thinking that Christ is insufficient for all of life. The hope of the gospel is the confident expectation in Jesus Christ to express His character through me in my everyday life.

The Hope Laid Up for You in Heaven

We are barely five verses deep into the letter when we are first introduced to hope. Paul is grateful to God for the faith and love of these dear saints.

> We always thank God, the Father of our Lord Jesus Christ, when we pray for you, since we heard of your faith in Christ Jesus and of the love that you have for all the saints, *because of the hope* laid up for you in heaven (Colossians 1:3-5 ESV).

What does he mean by "because of the hope laid up for you in heaven"? Our introductory, blurry glimpse at hope will become more clearly focused further into the epistle. Hope here is not defined; that will come later. For now hope is simply introduced as a glorious cause of brotherly love, the blooming garden of love sprung forth out of the rich soil of hope.

Not Shifting from the Hope of the Gospel

Hope takes on additional clarity by its second reference. It is not just any hope, but "the hope of the gospel." The gospel is the message of good news of what God has done for us in Jesus Christ. Note that it is not the hope *in* the gospel, that is, hoping in the message itself, but the hope *of* the gospel, a hope which is Christ Himself, to which the message points.

Through the first 22 verses, Paul has been thanking, praying, and exalting Jesus Christ and what He has done. Then suddenly we get our first inklings of danger. Ominous storm clouds are gathering on the horizon.

> And you, who once were alienated and hostile in mind, doing evil deeds, he has now reconciled in his body of flesh by his death, in order to present you holy and blameless and above reproach before him, if indeed you continue in the faith, stable and steadfast, *not shifting [metakineo] from the hope of the gospel that you heard* (Colossians 1:21-23 ESV).

Metakineo (meh-tah-kee-NEH-oh) is an interesting Greek word that means to move or shift from one place to another. It also means to shake and shift off, as used picturesquely in the Septuagint translation of Isaiah:

> "For the mountains may depart and the hills be removed [*metakineo*], but my steadfast love shall not depart from you, and my covenant of peace shall not be removed," says the LORD, who has compassion on you (Isaiah 54:10 ESV).

Shifting is also in the passive voice, meaning that the Colossians were being acted upon by an outside force. Some external pressure was at work to shake and shift them off the firm hope they had received. The kingdom of darkness that God had rescued these saints from (Colossians 1:13) does not abandon its operations against its former prisoners.

Shifting in the present tense means that these forces were in continuous activity to shake and shift off the saints from their hope of the gospel. Paul will later identify these forces as the false teachers in Colossae. Satan, using human agencies, targets the hope of the gospel as his primary objective.

The real spiritual war is being waged against the *hope* of the gospel! The enemy seeks to shake and shift off our firm hope of the good news. Notice that the Spirit of God does not say, "shifted from *the gospel* that you heard," but says rather, "shifted from *the hope* of the gospel that you heard." The demonic hosts were fighting an uphill battle, but found a chink in the armor. The front line assault of satanic strategy was not directly upon the gospel itself—to turn these saints who had trusted in Christ to trust instead in Zeus or Caesar. It was to substitute a different, less powerful, less able to be trusted, less worthy of our hope, less sufficient, less preeminent Jesus.[11] This unique assault bypassed the objective facts of the gospel but aimed to corrupt the *confident expectation* these believers had in the hope of the gospel, the Lord Jesus. "Jesus is really great, just not everything. He's very tall, just not all."

Paul describes the Colossian saints like a formidable

---

[11] Much thanks goes to my editor friend, Rick Gallipeau, for this wording to convey the subtlety of this strategy!

Roman legion in battle formation. He says, "I am with you in spirit, rejoicing to see your *good order* and the *firmness* of your faith in Christ" (Colossians 2:5 ESV). *Good order* is a military term describing an orderly array of soldiers with the line being unbroken and intact. *Firmness* is another military term that describes a group of Roman soldiers arranged in an unbreakable square or immoveable phalanx with shields joined and long spears overlapping.[12] It presented a solid bulwark against the shock of the enemy's charge. Paul was rejoicing in such a unified and unyielding front of trust in the Lord Jesus. Yet this did not hinder the enemy from brazenly exerting pressure against the weak spot—the object of their hope. If a robust army of the Lord like the Colossians can be susceptible to these attacks to shift and shake them off "the hope of the gospel," the preeminent Christ, do we suppose that we're exempt from such bold attacks? Let's learn from Paul to remain alert and on our guard. It is through warnings that we will be presented complete and mature in Christ (Colossians 1:28).

Although we believe in Jesus Christ, the unconscious danger is the subtle erosion of hope in His present power for being victorious over the flesh. Diminishing hope makes us susceptible to so-called "Christian" teachings that actually lead us away from Christ and rob us of our treasures in Him.

Jesus Christ in You, the Hope of Glory

Thus far Paul has introduced hope as the catalyst for brotherly love. Then Paul shakes us awake with a violent thunderstorm, a spiritual conflict threatening to shake and

---

[12] "Phalanx," *Webster's Encyclopedic Unabridged Dictionary of the English Language* (Random House Value Publishing, Inc., New York, 1996) p. 1451

shift us off our hope of the gospel, Christ. We are now prepared to see hope in an even sharper focus as a Person. Although we subjectively experience it, hope, in its ultimate sense, is not a feeling or a thing, but a Person. This colossal Christ *is* our hope (1 Timothy 1:1), our "hope of glory."

> To [the saints] God chose to make known how great among the Gentiles are the riches of the glory of this mystery, which is *Christ in you,*[13] *the hope of glory* (Colossians 1:27 ESV).

Words, as we know, can have multiple meanings depending upon their context. Hope, as we experience it, is a positive expectation directed towards Jesus Christ. "There shall come the root of Jesse, and He who arises to rule over the Gentiles, in Him shall the Gentiles hope" (Romans 15:12). Hope firmly fastens itself to the new and everlasting King David from the root of Jesse. Our hope soars when the colossal, preeminent Lord Jesus Christ becomes the supreme object of our trust.

The misleading teachers held out a false hope of glory now by employing spiritual activities (e.g., Jewish feasts and Sabbaths), special visions, and commandments of men. These sounded plausible and wise, but they were nothing but empty promises of victory over the flesh. Contrary to these preachers, Paul presented the immensity of Jesus Christ as the unshakeable, immovable anchor of hope. Hope is God's strong tower, casting its refreshing shade across the whole landscape of the epistle, reaching

---

[13] The Greek for *you* is plural (i.e., you all), meaning Jesus in the whole community. What's true corporately is true individually. Christ is in me; He is also in His church, which is composed of individuals like you and me.

from earth to heaven—as touching earth, "Christ in you, the hope of glory;" as touching heaven, "the hope laid up for you in heaven" (Colossians 1:27, 5).

Christ alone is a safe haven from God's wrath for past sins and from defeat for present indwelling sin. Our hope of the gospel includes an all-inclusive package for dealing with sin past (sins forgiven), present (sins overcome), and future (sins annihilated). These supplemental teachings come as stealthy thieves to rob us of Christ's fullness for the needs of the present hour.

No doubt Jesus Christ is the hope of the glory to come in the not-so-distant future—at the end of all the ages at His promised return. That is a passion of Paul's heart—but not what he is laboring to emphasize here. In writing this letter to real group of discouraged believers, what the Spirit of God inspired through Paul is hope *now*. It is of utmost importance that we see that Christ is the hope of glory now, in the present evil age where we are faced with dangers within and dangers without.

Faith surveys Jesus Christ as an immense universe and receives Him as the help in time of need. Hope is the favorable expectation that Jesus will exercise His power today. Closely connected with the believer's hope is God's willingness. Though we may be absolutely confident in God's ability, doubting His willingness pours cold water on the flames of hope. The leper that came to Jesus had a rock-solid assurance in His ability to cleanse him of his leprosy. What he lacked, though, was an assurance of His willingness.

> While He was in one of the cities, behold, there was a man covered with leprosy; and when he saw Jesus, he fell on his face and implored Him, saying, "Lord, if You are willing, You can make me clean." And He stretched out His hand and touched him, saying, "I am willing; be

cleansed." And immediately the leprosy left him (Luke 5:12-13).

Understanding that God is not only able but willing is the fuel that ignites our hope. Hope flourishes, not because we know God is able, but because we trust that God has both the power *and* the willingness to do it. His eagerness is what anchors our hope in the objective reality of truth, not just wishful thinking. Paul prays to secure our confidence in understanding how desirous God is to enable us to live in a well-pleasing way. Just as God made Jesus Christ preeminent in the natural universe, He delights to make Him preeminent in our spiritual lives, too.

So Paul shared how he prayed for them, specifically that God would help them understand His will.

> For this reason also, since the day we heard of it, we have not ceased to pray for you and to ask that you may be filled with the knowledge of His will in all spiritual wisdom and understanding (Colossians 1:9).

God's will is an immensely broad topic. As we look through the narrow lens of Colossians, God's will is that Christ be everything, that Christ be all and in all. What Paul had first prayed about, now he's writing about: "To whom God *willed to make known* what is the riches of the glory of this mystery among the Gentiles, which is Christ in you, the hope of glory" (Colossians 1:27). God wants you to know that Christ *is* the hope of glory. God wants us to know that He's willing for us to experience His riches now in His Son.

Hope Heals the Discouraged Heart
We need in our day what these discouraged believers in

Colossae needed in theirs. Hope is the cure for discouragement, especially a hope in the present power of Christ. As our hope in the Christ of the message of God's grace diminishes, our attraction to other messages that actually lead us away from Christ increases. We become more susceptible to being swept along by the undertow of the "Do more! Try harder!" preaching of our day. I find often that the "preacher" is my own mind, not completely freed from its natural bent towards self-effort (legalism). Only hope in Jesus Christ offers real help to "walk in a manner worthy of the Lord, to please Him in all respects, bearing fruit in every good work" (Colossians 1:10).

Paul preached Christ, being rooted in Him, built up in Him, holding fast to Him, seeking and minding Christ as the supreme focal point. Heeding God's wisdom, the gospel, is the fertile field in which the Gardener yields His choicest fruits. God the Father will manifest His Son as He truly is to the seeking heart, and in so revealing Him, imparting overcoming power and glory of eternal life!

Hope steers our discouragement away from hollow religiosity or overtaxing church busyness towards Jesus Christ, the hope of overflowing, abounding glory. Having our hope fixed in something other than Christ leads to devastating consequences. What we need to put our flesh to death here and now is *life*—not rules, religious programs, severe treatment of the body, a busy church schedule, saturation with Christian service, or insulating ourselves from the world with Christian fellowship.

Hope anchored in the present power of Christ answers our yearning for liberation from the present power of indwelling sin. The Promiser will come, as the Father wills to reveal Him through the gospel, and produce every fruit that pleases God in the here and now, as well as the life to come. Christ is our life! He is enough! He is all we need!

God delights to overwhelmingly, abundantly supply Christ, the hope of glory, our inherited life every day, all day.

Part 2

The Glorious Riches of Christ's Fullness is Power for Holiness Today

CHAPTER 6

Paul's Secret

In Part 1, "Diagnosing Doubt and Discouragement: Amnesia in a Jesus Universe," we observed how Paul homed in on the root problem plaguing this faithful group of Colossian believers. In many ways they were very commendable, full of love, faith, and unity, but they were a discouraged lot because their walk wasn't going so great. Enemies in the heavenly realms were continually at work to shift and shake them off the hope of the gospel—not to abandon Jesus Christ, but to diminish their expectation of His willingness to help them in the here and now. These temptations ganged up on them to distract their focus from Jesus Christ to many things related to Him. The main One was no longer the main One.

Compounded with their discouragement were symptoms of spiritual amnesia about how radically their lives were changed when they first received Christ Jesus the Lord. Paul reminded them of how Jesus was the beginning, the pivotal factor in the cleaning up the scum of all their nature and filling up their lives with faith and love. He called attention to how they were living in a Jesus universe, saturated with His preeminence in creation and in the church. This colossal Christ that they'd received at the start is also their hope of glory. Hope soars on eagles' wings when the unrivaled object of trust is preeminently Jesus.

In Part 2, "The Glorious Riches of Christ's Fullness is Power for Holiness Today," we continue tracing out the contours of Paul's progressive logic in the Colossian letter. Paul was itching to divulge to these distressed believers an astounding secret that God had revealed to him. This secret is a key to entering into the fabulous riches of the fullness of Christ in which each believer has a share.

He'll take the hope of glory to a new level, to the present power of Christ demonstrated in our lives in the cruddy here and now. The Jesus who will be glorious when He comes again is the same Jesus who is glorious now. Although His glory today will be to a far lesser degree, nevertheless it is a magnificent degree. So don't neglect the now, because He's the One who was, who is, and is to come. He doesn't want us to miss out on any part of who He is. Praise God that He is the One to come, but He also is the I am, the One who is! The Father is everlastingly poised to reveal Christ's glory in our lives today and tomorrow and when He comes again and through eternity.

A Steward of the Mysteries

God revealed an ancient secret to Paul. Abel the sacrifice presenter, Noah the ark builder, Abraham the friend of God, Moses the law-giver, David the sweet psalmist of Israel, Jeremiah the weeping prophet, and Nehemiah the wall builder all were unaware of it. This secret was the key to unlocking the door to the true riches the Colossians were searching for in all the wrong places. Now that Paul has guided us through a few mountainous peaks of the jaw-dropping wonders of the person and work of the Lord Jesus Christ, he's ready to let us in on this age-old secret to dispel our present discouragement.

> Now I rejoice in my sufferings for your sake, and in my flesh I do my share on behalf of His body, which is the church, in filling up what is lacking in Christ's afflictions. Of this church I was made a minister according to the stewardship from God bestowed on me for your benefit, so that I might fully carry out the preaching of the word of God, that is, the mystery which has been hidden from the past ages and generations, but has now been manifested to His saints, to whom God willed to make known what is the riches of the glory of this mystery among the Gentiles, which is Christ in you, the hope of glory (Colossians 1:24-27).

One big thought that catches our attention here is the word *mystery*. When we think of mystery, we often think from the perspective of not knowing what the outcome is going to be, such as a murder mystery. It connotes this dark, veiled curtain, like the one in the classic movie, *The Wizard of Oz*. In the Greek it doesn't mean that; mystery is an open secret. It has 20-20 hindsight after the curtain has been opened, like at the end of *The Wizard of Oz* when the seemingly great and terrible Oz is exposed as an unimposing pipsqueak of a man.

In connection with mystery, Paul conveys that he "was made a minister according to the stewardship from God." Another translation for *stewardship* is "dispensation," in the sense of a steward entrusted with dispensing according to his master's wishes. A steward doesn't own the treasures; he's just in charge of dispensing them. Paul says elsewhere, "Let a man regard us in this manner, as servants of Christ and stewards of the mysteries of God" (1 Corinthians 4:1). Paul's stewardship consisted of dishing out "the word of God, that is, the mystery which has been hidden...which is Christ in you, the hope of glory."

The mystery that Paul was entrusted with was for millennia cloaked and hidden. "The mystery...has been hidden from the past ages and generations, but now has been manifested to His saints" (Colossians 1:26). So there were epochs when this mystery of Jesus Christ, the hope of glory, being in the Gentiles and Jews wasn't known. After Jesus came, the cover was removed, and Paul was commissioned as a steward over this open secret.

This mystery is explained in terms of riches. "God willed to make known what is the riches of the glory of this mystery." So this mystery, this open secret, is God's wealth. It's His treasury, His storehouse of unfathomable riches. Paul's Colossian letter, as an avenue of his stewardship, dispenses and makes available that wealth to all of us to likewise see and partake of. He's distributing the treasury of God, the person of Jesus Christ. So what dispels discouragement is this open secret: Christ in you, the hope of glory, the hope of the gospel to which you and I are to cling.

A University Degree in Christ

As we cross the border into chapter 2, we meet these other teachers in Colossae, the front line soldiers skirmishing over the hope of the gospel. These were the pawns of invisible principalities and powers on a sinister mission to instill doubt that Jesus alone is the source of holiness today.

Those having Jewish roots were peddling circumcision, food and festival observances, and stuff like that. "If you're not doing these, you're disqualified; you'll never amount to much in God's perspective." You also had the Gnostic types who held that material things were evil and spiritual things were good. They promoted these supposedly super-spiritual revelations and visions of angels. Paul's paraphrased rebuttal is, "Those guys don't have the treasures. God has entrusted me as a steward of the mysteries to dispense the true riches to His people."

Paul prays passionately in accordance with God's desire for His people to know "what is the riches of the glory of this mystery," this open secret of His storehouse of unsearchable riches in Christ:

> For I want you to know how great a struggle I have on your behalf and for those who are at Laodicea, and for all those who have not personally seen my face, that their hearts may be encouraged, having been knit together in love, and attaining to all the wealth that comes from the full assurance of understanding, resulting in a true knowledge of God's mystery, that is, Christ Himself, in whom are hidden all the treasures of wisdom and knowledge (Colossians 2:1-3).

The opposite of *full assurance* is doubt. Paul prayed that they would abound in a full assurance, a perfect confidence or freedom from doubt, that every real treasure is in the Lord Jesus. With an unflinching confidence like that, the counterfeit treasures offered on the basis of earthly wisdom lose all appeal. In Jesus, God's best mystery, is hidden all the treasures of wisdom and knowledge. If *all* the treasures are hidden in Him, then why go anywhere else? These other messages actually take you away from the treasures.

Paul buttresses his defense by alluding back to Epaphras, the hometown evangelist who first preached the gospel of grace.

> Rooted and built up in Him and established in the faith, *as you have been taught* (Colossians 2:7 NKJV).

What you were originally taught is what you need. You don't need these trendy fads from the new teachers who blew into town. You've already got the best. God didn't leave out or forget anything you needed. It's all there.

So Paul goes head-to-head with the false teachers, who are still all around today. They're gift-wrapped differently in our twenty-first century, but underneath the shiny paper is the same spirit. There's nothing new under the sun. Paul picturesquely portrays these other philosophers as robbers:

> Beware lest anyone cheat [*sylagōgeō*] you through philosophy and empty deceit, according to the tradition of men, according to the basic principles of the world, and not according to Christ (Colossians 2:8 NKJV).

Cheat is *sylagōgeō* (soo-lah-goh-GEH-oh), which means to carry away captive or to plunder the spoils obtained by a victory in battle. Both meanings are very applicable here. These so-called philosophers offer a wealth of wisdom but actually plunder the Christian's treasure chest—Christ. Paying attention to these *basic principles of the world* leaves one impoverished, powerless to walk in a manner that's worthy of the Lord. The end result is that these Christ-deserting philosophies enslave the Christian, leaving him spiritually destitute. So beware, be on the lookout, because these philosophies and empty deceits will carry you away into bondage. They promise freedom. They promise to relieve your discouragement by achieving this morality, but they'll actually have the opposite effect of leading you into slavery to sin. Instead of finding true freedom in Jesus Christ as at the beginning, the bondage of works and legalism stealthily takes over.

The zenith of Paul's closing argument against his opponents is the worthlessness of their wisdom.

> These have indeed an appearance of wisdom in promoting self-made religion and asceticism and severity to the body, but they are of no value in stopping the indulgence of the flesh (Colossians 2:23 ESV).

Sitting down at the breakfast table and staring down a bowl of Fruit Loops to build up your resistance to temptation is not going to help. All of these pragmatic things may seem to be the answer to controlling your flesh, but Paul's assessment is they have zero value against the indulgence of the flesh. The Greek word for *value* is *timē* (tee-MAY), meaning value, price, or honor. All these teachings that try to supplement the gospel are worthless. Like a counterfeit diamond, they looked pricey, but really were throwaways for the garbage dump in comparison with the unmatchable, unsearchable riches of Christ. It is Christ "in whom are hidden all the treasures of wisdom and knowledge" (Colossians 2:3).

The message of Colossians is so fresh today because if it's not the false teachers redirecting our focus away from Christ, it's us. We get discouraged and think, "Well, maybe the gospel's not working. Maybe I need to set a regimen and discipline my flesh better to get it under control. That's the solution." While discipline is important, it is not the centerpiece. Christ being everything is the nucleus.

When you find yourself failing in some area, you don't need to go outside of Christ. If you're watching too much television, is there wisdom in applying "touch not" by turning the TV set off? Sure there is. But stopping the indulgence of the flesh doesn't come from turning the TV off. You can turn the TV, radio, smartphone, and all these things off, but if it's according to the basic principles of the world and not according to Christ, it has no value for curbing your fleshly excesses.

We can invent all these touch not, taste not holiness rules to try to protect ourselves from our flesh. "I'm not going to the beach because I'll get tempted to lust after all those bikini-clad women." Should you not go to the beach? Maybe you shouldn't. But if you think your rule, "Touch not the beach," makes you holy and subdues your flesh, you're being carried away captive through philosophy and empty deceit. If you avoid the beach because you're responding to promptings from the life of Christ within, you're following Paul's lead. "I'll get an Internet filter so it will stop me from going to bad websites." Is that okay? It is if you're not trusting in that. But what about the filter of the Holy Spirit? If He's living in you, He'll do far exceedingly better than any filter you have that's after the flesh.

We can institute a lot of these kinds of rules and regulations for ourselves or even others. Can there be a place for them? Yes, *as long as* we're not looking to them for life. We're to hold fast to the Head, Christ, who is our life. We're not to be shifted and shaken off the hope of the gospel. That's not to say there isn't wisdom in applying a man-made rule, because the fullness of wisdom in Christ may express itself that way in our lives. Paul's point is,

"Don't divert your attention and affection from Jesus. He's where we get our life." If we're failing, it's not coming up with new rules and 12-step programs; it's look to Christ. As you started, that's how you continue and how you finish. You received Christ by faith as a helpless sinner at the beginning, and you keep on receiving Christ by faith as a helpless saint. Our progress in the faith is no different from our beginning. As you received Christ Jesus the Lord, so walk in Him. It's that simple.

So Paul dispels the notion that you need some other message to make the gospel really work for you. When you received Christ, you received everything. That's what chapter 1 was all about. You received the Creator of the whole universe and Sustainer of all life, who holds everything together—including your spiritual life. You didn't receive some inferior "angel Jesus." So stay rooted in the Savior. You don't need to look outside of Jesus for life.

God, who graciously gives us Jesus, wants us to know that He is available to display His glory through us *now*. So if we're having problems in our Christian walk *now*, follow Paul's example laid out here in this Colossian epistle. If you have problems downstairs, you just need to go upstairs and take a look at everything that's true. That's what Paul, as a steward dispensing the riches of God's open secret, does in chapters 1 and 2: "Let me take you upstairs and show you what awesome and amazing things Christ did! He created everything there is in the whole universe! He's the firstborn from the dead! He reconciled you through His blood! All things in this material universe, whether great or small, whether visible or invisible, are held together by Him. How much more will He hold together your spiritual life." So if you're having problems walking your Christian walk down here, you need to be looking upstairs. That's the solution. The solution is seeing true facts of what God has done for you in Christ to ignite your faith.

CHAPTER 7
Fullness in Christ

How is a Christian to consistently bear fruit to God? The Colossians' discouragement centered upon this question. Paul succinctly frames his answer in the epistle's key verse: "Therefore as you have received Christ Jesus the Lord, so walk in Him" (Colossians 2:6). What are chapters 1 and 2? You received Christ. What are chapters 3 and 4? So walk in Him. Our walking in Christ depends on receiving Christ. How did you receive Christ at the beginning? It was grace, it was a gift. As Charles Rolls put it,

> Christ as a Gift cannot be obtained by some great performance on man's part, or merited by virtue of any human magnificence; nor is He secured by monetary payment however great. He is a Gift to be received.[14]

---

[14] Charles J. Rolls, *The Indescribable Christ: Names and Titles of Jesus Christ A - G* (Neptune, New Jersey: Loizeaux Brothers, 1983), p. 184

This Gift came to you through the Holy Spirit's quickening of the word of God shared with you by messengers like Epaphras. Paul comes as another messenger, a God-ordained dispenser of the open secrets of the riches of heaven, revealing God's heart and will. Expanding on the key verse, Paul shows just how full believers are in the superabundance of Jesus Christ:

> Therefore as you have received Christ Jesus the Lord, so walk in Him, having been firmly rooted and now being built up in Him and established in your faith, just as you were instructed, and overflowing with gratitude (Colossians 2:6-7).

Having been firmly rooted and *being built up* are both passive, meaning that these are not actions we do but someone else does for us. That someone is God, who in Christ rooted us and is building us up. Back in chapter 1, Paul explained how the Father "rescued us from the domain of darkness, and transferred us to the kingdom of His beloved Son" (Colossians 1:13). So the heavenly Gardener transplanted us, rooted us, in Christ. God is also the One who is building us up in Him. That's grace—God at work.

Paul uses a mixed metaphor of agriculture and architecture: "rooted and built up in Him" (NKJV). *Rooted in Him* suggests we as a tree are rooted into Christ as the ground. In nature roots are incredibly amazing! The plant world dazzles the imagination with the creative diversity of roots from the entangled web of aerial roots like the mangrove in the bayou to tuberous roots like potatoes to taproots drilling down to the depths. Some desert species of plants like the acacia tree have taproots penetrating as deep as 200 feet to reach water! In addition to their tenacious anchoring ability, incredible water absorption capabilities, and even strength to split rocks open, roots provide the food storage essential for their survival. Roots stockpile the food necessary to sustain the tree's existence during the harsh winter when its leaves are gone. When our Creator designed roots, He knew He would use them to illustrate our relationship with Himself. Roots point to the spiritual reality of our hearts seeking out, tapping into, and clinging tenaciously to Christ. Every tree and plant on our planet is silently telling the story of a believer's union with the Lord Jesus.

I've meditated on this a lot. Often when I come into my office building, I see several leafy trees standing as sentinels and am reminded that I am rooted in Christ. Just as the ground brings everything to the tree through its root system, Christ will bring everything to me. I often breathe a short prayer, "Lord, be preeminent to me today as the soil is to that tree."

You'll bear fruit if you stay rooted in your Soil, and you can't get any better soil than Jesus. As you look upstairs and see what Christ has done for you in the gospel, fruit automatically happens, just as your initial reception of the gospel had the pleasurable result of "constantly bearing fruit and increasing" (Colossians 1:6). Fruit will be produced as we're firmly rooted in the One who produces the fruit.

Built up is an architectural metaphor that means putting a roof on top of a building. In keeping with our agricultural theme, this translates to the above ground growing and producing fruit. *Rooted*, like the unseen roots of the tree, speaks of your hidden life—what you're receiving from God that no one sees. *Built up* speaks of your outer life—your words and actions for all to see. Your inner life (your roots) and outer life (your fruit) are both enriched in Jesus.

You are Full in Christ

When a sin problem alarms us, we can go one of two directions. Maybe you get angry a lot, frustrated a lot, worried a lot, depressed a lot, or whatever it is. You start to think, "Well, maybe if I just had these books or I followed these steps.... Maybe if I fasted ten times a week.... That would really help." Paul offers this counsel instead: "Take a look upstairs. You're already full."

> For in Him all the fullness of Deity dwells in bodily form, and in Him you have been made complete, and He is the head over all rule and authority (Colossians 2:9-10).

The ESV catches the original language of "in Him you have been made complete" a little better: "you have been filled in him." *Filled* is a close cousin of the Greek word translated *fullness* in the phrase, "all the fullness of Deity." The original Greek readers would have immediately seen the connection between their being filled and the fullness of Deity. I like the literal rendition: "you are in Him, having been filled."[15] *Having been filled* is in the Greek perfect tense, which means something that happened in the past that has on-going results to the present. For example, I was married on a certain date and I'm still married. The perfect tense has that thought. So we were filled when we first received Christ and have remained in a state of fullness to this present moment. So not only has the Father rooted you in Christ and is building you up in Christ, but has also filled you in Christ, a fullness that has not abated to the present moment.

---

[15] Green, Jay P., *Pocket Interlinear New Testament* (Grand Rapids, Michigan: Baker Book House, 1988), p. 544

To these downhearted Christians who felt that they weren't full, Paul testifies, "You're already full because you are in Christ, in whom all God's fullness lives." You are not running on empty because of these sins you're experiencing. Your being full is not dependent on how you're doing but on what God has done by firmly rooting you into His Son, in whom dwells all the fullness of Deity. So you *are* full.

Now we know that not every Christian appropriates his or her fullness in Christ the same way. One could still live as a beggar even though he has millions of dollars in the bank. Paul will explain how to appropriate that fullness in chapter 3, but first we need to see that we are already full. His admonishment there for us to put off fornication, uncleanness, and other sins cropping up are all possible because we are already full in Christ. Paul has a similar sentiment in his letter to the Ephesians: "Blessed be the God and Father of our Lord Jesus Christ, who has blessed us with every spiritual blessing in the heavenly places in Christ" (Ephesians 1:3). You have already been blessed with every spiritual blessing; you are already full in Christ.

Jesus has all the fullness of the Godhead bodily, so all of the Father you ever need is in Him. All of the fullness of the Holy Spirit is all there in Christ.

> "If anyone is thirsty," Jesus cried out, "let him come to Me and drink. He who believes in Me, as the Scripture said, 'From his innermost being will flow rivers of living water.'" But this He spoke of the Spirit, whom those who believed in Him were to receive (John 7:37-39).

So if you're coming to Christ, the reservoir from which gush the rivers of God's fullness, you have everything you need. Christ meets every need because He has all supply, and not just any supply—it's the fullness of God:

He is the beginning, the firstborn from the dead, so that He Himself will come to have first place in everything. For it was the Father's good pleasure for all the fullness to dwell in Him (Colossians 1:18-19 ESV).

The Father delights to have all His infinite, limitless presence dwelling in Jesus, the true temple, the meeting place between God and His people. Solomon's temple, for all its magnificence and splendor, contained only a miniature representation of the presence of God—the glorious pillar of cloud. Solomon's temple didn't house all the fullness, for Solomon himself declared,

But will God indeed dwell with mankind on the earth? Behold, heaven and the highest heaven cannot contain You; how much less this house which I have built (2 Chronicles 6:18).

What heaven and the highest heaven failed to enclose, Jesus can! Jesus as God the Son is the superior temple, for He transcends the entire universe—the starry heavens with its billions of galaxies that He made—and astonishingly contains all that God infinitely is. The good news is you've already been filled and are full in Christ, in whom the entirety of the Trinity dwells. So you don't need to seek elsewhere, because everything is all there in Him. Everything.

"God willed to make known what is the riches of the glory of this mystery among the Gentiles, which is Christ in you, the hope of glory" (Colossians 1:27). This open secret is God's storehouse of unsearchable riches in the person of Jesus as this universe-surpassing temple. Your fullness has nothing to do with your performance. So with this colossal, preeminent kind of Jesus that God has rooted us in, built us up in, and filled us in, we'll naturally bear fruit. So just relax and enjoy Christ!

Pictures of Grace

Paul then proceeds to pull out all the stops to show us God's amazing miracles on our behalf when we were dead in our trespasses and sins, deserving nothing but His wrath and indignation.

> In Him you were also circumcised with a circumcision made without hands, in the removal of the body of the flesh by the circumcision of Christ; having been buried with Him in baptism, in which you were also raised up with Him through faith in the working of God, who raised Him from the dead. When you were dead in your transgressions and the uncircumcision of your flesh, He made you alive together with Him, having forgiven us all our transgressions, having canceled out the certificate of debt consisting of decrees against us, which was hostile to us; and He has taken it out of the way, having nailed it to the cross. When He had disarmed the rulers and authorities, He made a public display of them, having triumphed over them through Him (Colossians 2:11-15).

This beautiful passage is laden with pictures of grace. The first grace snapshot leading the list is you were circumcised *by the circumcision of Christ*. In the Old Testament, circumcision was an important covenant seal marked by the removal of a little piece of flesh, the male's foreskin. Here Paul speaks of a circumcision made without man's hands, pointing above to the work of Christ. True circumcision is "the removal [putting off, stripping away] of the body of the flesh." So, when we were born again, something was stripped off—the body of the flesh that once enslaved us to sin. Christ's supernatural work of circumcising our hearts from the whole body of sins far transcended the external ritual of removing one little piece of flesh.

Philippians develops what circumcision means to the Christian today.

> For we are the true circumcision, who worship in the Spirit of God and glory in Christ Jesus and put no confidence in the flesh (Philippians 3:3).

Circumcision is worshiping, not at the correct geographical spot like Jerusalem or some mountain, as Jesus explained to the Samaritan woman at the well, but in the Spirit of God. Flesh and falsehood have been cut away that we may worship God in Spirit and in truth.

True circumcision is characterized by glorying in Christ Jesus' law-keeping and perfect performance deposited in your spiritual "bank account," not the bankruptcy that your incomplete, defective performance brings on. Some reinforced fleshly confidence by preaching circumcision as one's acceptance in God's sight. All these little rules and regulations that people pressure you into to be more spiritual or holy just aren't going to do it. You have to look back on these grace snapshots of what Jesus has done.

We won't expound in detail on every picture in Paul's densely packed grace mosaic here in chapter 2, but let's take a peek at Jesus' sin-forgiving work on the cross:

> When you were dead in your transgressions and the uncircumcision of your flesh, He made you alive together with Him, having forgiven us all our transgressions, having

canceled out the certificate of debt consisting of decrees against us, which was hostile to us; and He has taken it out of the way, having nailed it to the cross (Colossians 2:13-14).

How can you displease God if He's forgiven you of all your sins? "All our transgressions" means all. It means the sins you committed in the past, the sins that you committed today, and every sin that you will commit in the future. Keep in mind that when Jesus died for your sins 2,000 years ago, they were *all* in the future. There's no need for some purgatory after you die for you to suffer for sins that Jesus' death somehow missed out on. Jesus died for every sin. All your sins were buried with Jesus when you were "buried with Him in baptism." That relates back to the circumcision of Christ that stripped away the body of the flesh that once enslaved us.

He's taken away all our guilty sins against a holy God and nailed them to the cross! Every blot on our record Christ has paid for in full on Calvary. So God has nothing negative to say about us because He sees us perfected in His Son.

Now God does discipline us as a father who loves us, using providence and people, but not as a judge who sentences us to condemnation. Yes, the Bible speaks of a future judgment where believers' words and works will be tested and tried. Those are different teachings for another time. But before you can understand those, you must first fill your mind with these amazing pictures of grace.

Holding Fast the Head

One of Paul's favorite metaphors of Christ and the church is the head and the body. Now he's going to show the fullness and riches we have in Christ from a slightly different angle, a wealth expressed as nourishing life that the head furnishes to the whole body.

> Let no one keep defrauding you of your prize by delighting in self-abasement and the worship of the angels, taking his stand on visions he has seen, inflated without cause by his fleshly mind, and not holding fast to the head, from whom the entire body, being supplied and held together by the joints and ligaments, grows with a growth which is from God (Colossians 2:18-19).

We need to hold fast to the Head, the Lord Jesus. Your head controls everything, from the unconscious beating of your heart to the deliberate coordination of your hands and fingers, feet and toes. If you lose your arm or leg, though it would be a great handicap, you could still live. But without the head, the body is dead. I've never seen anybody without a head who did very well in life. To get an inkling of just how infinitely superior Christ as Head of His body must be, consider this panorama by Charles Rolls:

> When we consider the myriads to whom He ministers, which include all the saintly scholars, wise counselors, prominent leaders, eminent expositors, true teachers, excellent evangelists, sympathetic shepherds, missionaries of merit, tireless translators, worthy workers, memorable martyrs, and all the hosts which make up the innumerable multitude, how wonderful must Christ be, to be Head of such a tremendous concourse of saints![16]

---

[16] Charles J. Rolls, *The World's Greatest Name: Names and Titles of Jesus Christ H - K* (Neptune, New Jersey: Loizeaux Brothers, 1984), p. 26

So we hold fast to Jesus as our Head, just like our body adheres to its head. Paralysis happens because there's something out of sync between my head and my disabled limb. But as long as the connectivity to the brain is there, my arm or leg will do everything that the head wants. So what does the body do? The body just lives. The hand just responds to the impulses it gets from the head. Jesus' life will fill and animate each member of His body in union with Him as the Head. That's the confidence we can have. That's why we don't need a bunch of rules and regulations. We get our life from Jesus. Life is not something He gives us separate and distinct from Himself, but He Himself is that life. When Jesus declared, "I am the way, the truth, and the life," He meant just that. So we don't need more laws, we need Christ our life. Life provides all that's needed.

For over fifteen years, I used to think along these lines: *Since I live in a yucky world and I have yucky flesh, if I jam my schedule with church activities, then my flesh won't get into trouble and I can really be holy.* Certainly prayer, gathering with the body, and organized evangelism are good things, but they are not the center; they're the fruit. If we stay connected to our Head, Christ, the wonderful life of prayer, fellowship, and service will be automatic byproducts.

Leprosy is a disease that deadens the skin so that it's insensitive to everything. Lepers in some parts of the world actually have to check their feet at the end of the day for thorns. They have to have a rule: check your feet for splinters and thorns. But as soon as we step on a thorn, our foot immediate reacts. Because our foot has life in it, there's a sensitivity from the inside, so we don't need an external rule or regulation.[17] Likewise when we're holding

---

[17] I am appreciative of Zac Poonen, a Bible teacher from India, who introduced me many years ago to this simple analogy that has helped me to discern the difference between laws and life.

fast to the Head, Christ's Spirit gives us a sensitivity to the little thorns of sin that prick us, so we don't need rules. So what should be our focus? Take Paul's advice: revel in and enjoy Jesus, in whom dwells all the fullness of the Godhead bodily. Let faith be constantly directed toward one object, "fixing our eyes on Jesus, the author and perfecter of faith" (Hebrews 12:2). Believe that you've got all the fullness now. God wants you to experience your fullness in Christ, the hope of glory, now. So don't be moved away from the hope of the gospel, because He delights to manifest Christ in your life today.

Paul has ransacked the universe for metaphors and analogies to convey this amazing gospel you've received: a colossal Christ, Creator of everything. He's your soil, your fruit, your fullness, your circumciser, your substitute, your triumphant conqueror, your head, and so much more! Paul is taking you through the divine scrapbook, saying, "Hey, look at these pictures—here, here, here, here, here. Once you see what God did for you in Christ Jesus, everything else you're all discouraged about will fall into place." He directs you to relax in your easy chair and let all these pictures of grace soak in before he gets into commands for daily living. If you put the scrapbook away in some closet and forget about it, that's how all these other teachers will captivate your interest and attention and take you away captive.

CHAPTER 8

The Present Power of Christ

The classic Pixar digital animation film for children, *Cars*, features a braggadocios, cherry-red race car named Lightning McQueen. McQueen dreams of winning the Piston Cup to become the number one race car with all its fame and fortune. During the final lap of the race, in order to save time, Lightning McQueen risks not making a pit stop to replace his well-worn tires. His gamble fails and both rear tires blow out as the black and white checkered flag waves in sight. In a desperate struggle to reach the finish line, the rims scrape and spark the last yards as McQueen snails along at a sluggish pace. The two lagging competitors quickly catch up and the race ends in a dramatic three-way tie.

If we're not careful, we can miss the heart of the book of Colossians and be like Lightning McQueen on our highway of holiness, spinning our wheels with great energy but with little forward progress. Paul has painstakingly labored to thoroughly ground our hope in a colossal Christ, yet in spite of all this, our progress in holiness can be slowed to a crawl going into the home stretch of Colossians 3 and 4. These pivotal verses bridging the doctrines of chapters 1 and 2 with the day-to-day practical living it out in chapters 3 and 4 can, without our realizing it, lose their intended force:

> Therefore if you have been raised up with Christ, keep seeking the things above, where Christ is, seated at the right hand of God. Set your mind on the things above, not on the things that are on earth. For you have died and your life is hidden with Christ in God. When Christ, who is our life, is revealed, then you also will be revealed with Him in glory (Colossians 3:1-4).

Too often our rear tires blow out because the principles of Colossians 3:1-4, where the theology transitions to the practical, get blown out by importing other biblical texts to ascertain their meaning rather than the context in which they are found. The way we understand and apply the practical sections of Colossians still moves us forward, but with a tremendous loss of momentum. An incomplete understanding of these verses sucks the wind out of the sails of the hope of the gospel.

The language of "When Christ, who is our life, is revealed" inspires our imagination to the glories of Christ when He comes back again. The second coming is the supreme expression of Christ our life! Jesus, who is hidden from the eyes of the world, will be revealed again from heaven in glory. "Behold, He is coming with the clouds, and every eye will see Him" (Revelation 1:7). When we see Him, we shall be like Him (1 John 3:2). What a glorious truth that when Christ is revealed we will also be revealed with Him in glory!

But in light of the divine stream of logic developed

through the first two chapters of Colossians, is this how we are to interpret "When Christ, who is our life, is revealed"? Most Christ-loving expositors, whom I have greatly benefitted from and deeply respect, say this verse refers exclusively to Jesus Christ's second coming. But is this verse limited to one future climactic event or can it mean a continuous experience here and now? Paul did not spend two full chapters developing the supremacy of Christ Jesus to then suddenly develop amnesia coming into the third chapter. It is all one connected flow of the divine mind that Paul was privy to.

Though the second coming is in view, the carefully sculpted themes of Colossians 1 and 2 strongly advocate the omnipresence of Christ right now that impacts our everyday life. Think about the context that Paul is using it in, the hope of glory now. Crystallized in the imagery of Christ's second coming is a *principle* for daily life. Immediately following "When Christ, who is our life, is revealed" is this verse: "Therefore put to death your members which are on the earth." Is that for when Christ comes again? No, that's for right now! That phrase "put to death" is an imperative, a command, in a tense that means put to death right this minute.

By relegating "When Christ, who is our life, is revealed" to the second coming sometime in the future, the momentum of the first two chapters transfers from the tire (Christ our life) to the naked rim (our motivation). We can unintentionally minimize Christ's power to overcome sin and produce God-glorifying fruit in us today. I want to make sure that we don't unwittingly gloss over this Grand Canyon truth in understanding Colossians. If this is purely a future prophecy, it subtly postpones the power today until later, when Christ comes in glory in the clouds. We end up swapping the present power of Christ preeminent in our daily lives for a pep talk that excites desire and hope but not ability. Sorrowfully, sluggishness in the progress of our spiritual growth is the inevitable result. God has always intended our spiritual growth to be rooted in a preeminent Christ, not in our up-and-down motivations.

A New Motive of a New Power?

Some teach that before we were saved we didn't have the right motivation for being victorious over the sins of our flesh. But now that we are saved, we can obey God because of a new motive of love and thankfulness for what He has done for us. It is true that having a motive of love and gratitude for God is crucial in our obedience. 1 Corinthians 13 makes it very clear that without love everything we do is like a noisy, irritating gong.

Other Scriptures elsewhere testify that the knowledge of Christ's return is another factor that motivates us to purify our conduct. The apostle John wrote,

> We know that when He appears, we will be like Him, because we will see Him just as He is. And everyone who has this hope fixed on Him purifies himself, just as He is pure (1 John 3:2-3).

But what does the Colossian letter emphasize: a new motive or a new power? Does our being complete in Christ, in whom all the fullness of Deity dwells in bodily form, speak towards a new motivation or a new power? Colossians does address motivation, but mainly in terms of the Father's willingness, not ours. Hope for the discouraged heart is not first and foremost upon *our* motivation but upon *God's*. What dissipates our discouragement is a clear understanding of His willingness to make Christ preeminent in working out our salvation.

So motives do importantly factor into our obedience. The Colossians, though, were not motivationally challenged to clean up their behavior; their issue was that they were tempted to use the wrong soap! So in treating the delicate situation in Colossae, Paul's emphasis is upon the *present power* abundantly supplied according to revelation of the preeminence of Jesus Christ through the gospel. Because He is preeminent, He is the fountainhead of eternal life, whose streams include victory over sin and appealing displays of His life in our character. The preeminent Vine supplies all life to every branch united to Him. Christ's supremacy assures us of His power exerted everywhere, at every time, in every believer. Hope in the preeminent Lord Jesus is the key for appropriating Him today and every day. Our remaining fixed in the hope of this gospel is when radical change happens. Christ in you as a *hope* of glory back in Colossians 1:27 makes a fantastic advance:

> When Christ, who is our life, is revealed, then you also will be revealed with Him in glory (Colossians 3:4).

That unseen hope of glory wonderfully and amazingly transitions to actually possessing and enjoying the glory of God! It is the Father's will to elevate Christ in us as a *hope* for glory to Christ as a *revealing* of glory! Jesus in us, the hope of glory, shines out of us as glory—not as physical light or a halo over our heads, but a life characterized by love toward God and man. Take courage that your heavenly Father will see to it that Christ in you as a hope of glory ends with His glory being seen in your life. "Let your light shine before others, so that they may see your good works and give glory to your Father who is in heaven" (Matthew 5:16 ESV).

Receiving the promise of glory hoped for means perceptible glory in and through you today. Colossians 3 and 4 illustrate what this metamorphosis of a believer appearing with Jesus in glory looks like in practice. Chapter 3 sketches the glory of Christ in principles—putting off sin, putting on God's character qualities, and transforming our interpersonal relationships. Chapter 4 exhibits a trophy case of blood-bought sinners who experienced transformation through this message of Colossians. These are men with passions and frailties like ours who had embraced and held fast to the simple gospel message. Tychicus and Onesimus and Epaphras and Luke each showcase a variety of Christ's glories for our encouragement.

Christ's Preeminence: Appearing with Him in Glory
The themes of Colossians direct the believer to tap directly into the power source for living the Christian life. The all-pervading theme of the Lord Jesus Christ's preeminence in everything should significantly influence our comprehension of this verse:

> When Christ, who is our life, is revealed, then you also will be revealed with Him in glory (Colossians 3:4).

Drilling down a bit into the nuts and bolts of the original language will give us a better sense of how the Colossians would have understood this passage. Since this is the capstone verse transitioning from theology to practice, it's vital we don't miss what the Spirit is saying here. Both "revealed" verbs are in the passive voice:

> When Christ, who is our life, is revealed [passive], then you also will be revealed [passive] with Him in glory.

Passive voice means that the subject is being acted upon by someone or something else. So "when Christ, who is our life, is revealed" is not Jesus Christ openly showing Himself (i.e., active voice), rather, this is conducted by Another, namely God (i.e., passive voice). Another sense of the text using the active voice might read like this: "When God reveals Christ who is your life."

Our English rendering *revealed* misses out on some of the nuances of the Greek. The Greek *phaneroō* (fah-neh-RAH-oh) means to show openly something which had been hidden. But it goes even further than merely displaying something like a magician showing a white rabbit out of his top hat; it is a disclosure with understanding. To illustrate, when Judas betrayed the Lord Jesus in Gethsemane, to the soldiers and temple guards his kiss was a signal identifying whom they were to arrest. To the oblivious disciples, it appeared simply as a typical Jewish greeting. Both groups saw the same thing, but only one understood the true meaning behind it. *Phaneroō* would be what the soldiers and temple guards saw and understood.

So how do we appear with Jesus glory? Does He physically appear? "When Christ, who is our life, is revealed [*phaneroō*]" points to the manifestation of Christ our life that transcends mere human perception to the real meaning behind it. It could mean Christ actually visible, such as when He will appear on the clouds with great glory. In the context of Colossians, though, Paul has been championing Jesus Christ as the firstborn from the dead, "that He might become in all things Himself the one who is preeminent." That preeminence of Christ pervades the natural realms in many ways imperceptible to our five senses. Do we see His imperial control of myriads of unseen angels? Do we observe how the whole universe is held together by the word of His power? So our appearing with Christ in glory doesn't mean that a watching world will physically see a smiling, bearded Jesus with robe and sandals standing next to us. Rather, there is a spiritual reality to Christ's actually being manifested through us that is beyond what eyes can detect, as we will investigate.

The Greek word for *then* is *tote* (TAH-teh), an emphatic *then*, rarely used and only once in Colossians:

> When [or whenever[18]] Christ, who is our life, is revealed, then [*tote*] you will also be revealed with Him in glory.

Tote is intentionally selected when the author desires to make a conspicuously strong point about cause and effect. So when God reveals Christ, *then and only then*, will we appear in glory with Him. Thus, our appearing in glory (our walking in Him spelled out in chapters 3 and 4) is set in motion whenever the Father (or Spirit) reveals Christ to us. So our hope of transformation is anchored in the present power of Christ our life being revealed.

Christ's Glory is a Sin Killer

What proof do we have that we have appeared with Christ in glory? The first is victory over indwelling sin!

> Put to death therefore what is earthly in you: sexual immorality, impurity, passion, evil desire, and

---

[18] Greek *hotan* (HAW-tawn) can mean when or whenever and does not necessarily limit itself to a one-time event. For example, its first usage is Matthew 5:11 (ESV): "Blessed are you *when* [hotan] others revile you and persecute you and utter all kinds of evil against you falsely on my account."

covetousness, which is idolatry (Colossians 3:5 ESV).

Christ's glory is a sin killer. Sexual immorality is put to death as God manifests the glory of Christ through us. Though we are involved and responsible, the power of the putting to death is Christ's. Have you ever, like I have done, in looking for a quick fix for your flesh issues, reached into Colossians and yanked this verse out of context? "I'm going to fast breakfast and lunch so I can put to death this sin issue I'm having." And like a flower uprooted from its garden habitat, the spiritual life it intended to confer withers and dies. To yield the delectable fruit in our Christian lives necessitates that we explore the beauty of these words in the lush garden of verses in which they were divinely planted.

This *therefore* in "Put to death therefore" is one of those common conjunctions of cause and effect, the result or logical conclusion of that which preceded it. Our putting to death what is earthly in us is organically connected to the preceding verse regarding "Christ, who is our life, is revealed" and really the whole theme leading up to it from chapters 1 and 2. We need to pay careful attention to the *therefore* and understand, as the cliché says, what it's "there for."

Any attempt to put sin to death without holding fast the wider view of what God has already done for us in Jesus Christ (chapters 1 and 2) terminating in Christ's glory revealed to us (chapter 3) is a snare that the kingdom of darkness lays in our path. The gospel we heard at the beginning proclaims what God has done for us in Christ. We've died with Christ. We've been raised with Christ. We've ascended with Christ. We're seated with Christ in heavenly places. Because of all this, now God's ongoing work of grace is to make Christ appear to us in glory. This is what has immediate relevance towards putting sin to death and putting on Christ in the verses to follow.

We will now zoom out to consider the broader continuity of thought through this epistle. This *therefore* in "Put to death therefore" not only connects the preceding verses, but also forms the zenith of Paul's whole argument developed throughout chapter 2. The climax of his expose of the false teachers is this: they cannot deliver real and lasting results.

> These have indeed an appearance of wisdom in promoting self-made religion and asceticism and severity to the body, but they are of no value in stopping the indulgence of the flesh (Colossians 2:23 ESV).

So "Put to death therefore what is earthly in you" is placed in direct contrast to "no value in stopping the indulgence of the flesh." Whereas the false teachers' messages have no value to put to death the indulgence of the flesh—"what is earthly in you: sexual immorality, impurity, passion"—what Paul presents *does*. He confidently asserts that Christ being revealed does what no earthly commandment, festival, ascetic practice, philosophy, or other thing can achieve. Only God's pure grace, received through the revealing of Christ's glory in the gospel has value to put the flesh to death and bring about true character change. Christ alone is truly successful in putting sin to death and putting on us His own distinguishing attractiveness of love.

What's true in the future, Christ our life appearing at His second coming, has exciting implications for us today! God wills to manifest Christ our life now, just as at the second coming. The second coming will be the bursting grandeur and sky-saturating glory, but the principle is also true that Christ our life will appear right now. Every time Christ who *is* our life appears, we can expect what's earthly in us to be put to death. What puts our earthly passions to death is God manifesting Christ our life to us, not our reliance upon elementary principles (food and drink, Sabbaths, festivals) and commandments of men (touch not, taste not) that perish with the using. It's not by our effort; it's by Christ coming and appearing.

A truly heavenly mindset to "seek the things that are above" is the path to victory over sin. What keeps us from spinning our wheels like Lightning McQueen in our Christian race is seeking the things that are above, the topic of our next chapter. Our day-to-day practical living out the Christian life depends on rightly understanding and applying what Paul means to "seek the things that are above" that taps into the glory of Christ, the present power of God, our hope for holiness today.

CHAPTER 9

Seeking the Above

Christ is everything in Colossians chapter 1. He is the supreme originator and supplier of the universe and the church. In chapter 2, Paul refutes the erroneous notion that Jesus is not enough and establishes that He is God's treasury of wisdom and knowledge, in whom we have been filled with the fullness of Deity. Transformation occurs, not by human effort, but by faith in Christ's working. As chapter 3 turns the corner from doctrine to application, the almighty power of Jesus Christ comes today as a result of the Father revealing Him with us in glory.

We now turn to the important question, "Yes, but how?" How practically does the power and glory of Christ put to death the works of the flesh? How can I be more like Jesus? This question the discouraged Colossians wrestled with is a question of the ages. The daily practical how-to for us begins with Colossians 3:1-2:

> If then you have been raised with Christ, seek the things
> that are above, where Christ is, seated at the right hand
> of God. Set your minds on things that are above, not on

things that are on earth.

What exactly are *the things that are above* we to seek? That phrase has a broad, somewhat ambiguous meaning. We can fill in the blank for it to mean the kingdom of God, heaven, treasures in heaven, spiritual gifts, godly character, holy behavior, Jesus, Jesus' second coming, and so on. However, the preeminence of Jesus in the previous two chapters is the guardrail that prevents us from precariously veering off course here. Often Christians do not get this. I know I missed it for years. These verses so often go right over our heads because, as we discussed, we import meanings into them that are alien to the context of the letter. May God help us recover His excellent wisdom presented here for us!

When Paul enjoins us to "seek the things that are above," *things* has a hazy notion of stuff or a bunch of items, which presents a challenge in grasping the original train of thought. There is no word explicitly for *things* in here. The Greek is simply the definite article *the* combined with the word *ano* (AH-noh) for *above*, so it literally reads "the above." Similarly, Paul's other admonishment, "Set your minds...not on things that are on earth" is literally "the upon the earth," which sounds clunky in English, so *things* is inserted to make better sense. The insertion of *things* for similar constructions is usually a good translation into English; however, here I don't think it's the best because it leads our mind to think *stuff* whereas Paul's progressive train of thought runs along a different track, as we'll investigate shortly. I prefer to think "the above" and let the Spirit translate its contextual sense to my heart. From here on I will use the literal phrase "the above" interchangeably with "the things that are above" in order to direct our thinking more closely to the original recipients of this letter.

Things that are on Earth
In Little League baseball I learned that a key to successful batting is keeping my eye on the ball. Now that I'm a parent, in teaching my daughter or sons how to bat Wiffle balls on our village green, often after their swinging and missing, I remind them, "Keep your eye on the ball." If we don't know what Paul means to seek the things above, we may not have our eye on the ball and thereby miss God's help to dispel our discouragement in our spiritual walk. Many precious saints have inadvertently attributed their spiritual growth to other things, unconscious that their love for and attentiveness to what Paul meant by "the above" was the true cause. Thankfully God is exceedingly better than our theology of Him. Seeing through a glass darkly, none of us knows and understands God perfectly in this life. But we do want to keep our eye on the ball to avoid the pitfalls that Paul warns against.

The apostle has been building up a logical argument all through chapter 2. Through a careful reading of his line upon line, precept upon precept progression, we can get a better idea what is meant by "the above." To begin with, Paul sharply contrasts the content of his preaching against the other false teachers in Colossae.

> Him *we* proclaim, warning everyone and teaching everyone with all wisdom, that we may present everyone mature in Christ (Colossians 1:28 ESV).

The *we* in "Him we proclaim" is emphatic in Greek. Unlike English, which requires a pronoun with the main verb, in Greek (like Spanish) the pronoun is optional since the verb form implies it. So any time Greek inserts a pronoun, it is the author's intention to emphasize the I, he, she, we, they, or it. Paul is raising his voice a bit, declaring, "Him *we* proclaim," pointedly implying a *they*. As Paul contrasts what he preaches and teaches—Christ—with what the false teachers preach and teach, we see a number of references to the earth and the world, which taken together sum up the "things that are on earth." Watch how his opening argument pits teaching Christ against philosophical teachings and traditions according to principles of the world:

> See to it that no one takes you captive by philosophy and empty deceit, according to human tradition, *according to the elemental spirits [stoicheon] of the world*, and not according to Christ (Colossians 2:8 ESV).

The *elemental spirits* or "basic principles" (NKJV) is the Greek word *stoicheon* (stoi-KHI-on), derived from a verb for putting things in a row or arranging in order. Our alphabet illustrates this word well. The ABCs, for instance, are the basics of what young children learn first. Seniors in high school still aren't stuck on studying the alphabet, for their mastery of it has been assimilated into its higher purpose of reading and writing.

Paul debunks the false impression that these other teachings are so advanced, countering, "That's just kindergarten stuff; that's just ABCs. It's not according to Christ, in whom are all the treasures of wisdom and knowledge." If the teaching doesn't center itself in the person of Jesus Christ, it's just "the elemental spirits of the world." Every other philosophy, religion, or doctrine that infringes on the preeminence of Christ in order to promote human tradition in some way, shape, or form falls into the category of "things that are on earth."

Paul continues his assessment of the curriculum of the false teachers as being the simple beginnings, the earthly. He provides some examples of what he means by "elemental spirits":

> If you have died with Christ to the elementary principles [*stoicheon*] of the world, why, as if you were living in the world, do you submit yourself to decrees, such as, "Do not handle, do not taste, do not touch!" (which all refer to things destined to perish with use)—in accordance with the commandments and teachings of men? (Colossians 2:20-22).

Here Paul asserts that decrees, commandments, and teachings of men are *stoicheon*, the elemental or basic principles of the world that have no value in living the Christian life. In lumping the commandments and teachings of men in with the kindergarten basics, he is also contrasting their uninspired earthly origin against the divine revelation from heaven. Our having died with Christ means that we died to the elementary principles of the world—the ABCs of "Do not handle, do not taste, do not touch" and other man-made rules to curb your fleshly appetites. These are the "things that are on earth" that Paul warns us not to seek after.

Tripping Over Shadows
Though the Gnostics with their decrees, commandments, and super-special revelations are a serious problem, what really trips us up are those who use the Bible to bind us to the preparatory principles, "things that are on earth," rather than adhering to what's final and permanent in Christ:

Therefore no one is to act as your judge in regard to food or drink or in respect to a festival or a new moon or a Sabbath day—things which are a mere shadow of what is to come; but the substance belongs to Christ (Colossians 2:16-17).

The word for *substance* literally is "body," as in a human body. The silhouette of a person's shadow against the wall bears a striking resemblance to the person's body. All these Old Testament observances were like the shadows cast from the physique of their coming Messiah. These ceremonial observances were in essence the kindergarten basics to prepare the people for the main One, their long expected Messianic king and deliverer.

The Jews had all those dietary lists in Leviticus. If it has four hooves and chews the cud, it's kosher. If you eat these, you're spiritual. If you eat those, you're not. Paul addressed all these dietary controversies, summarizing, "For the kingdom of God is not eating and drinking, but righteousness and peace and joy in the Holy Spirit" (Romans 14:17). The Jewish dietary laws specifying clean and unclean animals were just an earthly shadow, an ABC, whose substance came in Jesus Christ. Peter's vision of a great sheet out of heaven filled with unclean animals stunningly announced that now these could be eaten because God had cleansed them (see Acts 10:9-16). Peter got that the principle of the vision was, "God has shown me that I should not call any man unholy or unclean" (Acts 10:28). Unclean animals foreshadowed the time when Christ's atoning work on Calvary would cleanse all classes of men—Jew and Gentile. So the food and drink prohibitions in the Old Testament are another example of the preparatory "things that are on earth" that lead us to the heavenly, spiritual reality in Christ.

The Jews also celebrated annual feasts (e.g., the Passover), the monthly observances (the new moon), and the weekly holy days (the sabbaths). The Sabbath as a day of rest dedicated from sundown Friday to sundown Saturday with all its prescribed rules and regulations under Mosaic Law has, as with food and drink, been swallowed up in the Lord Jesus Christ. "Come to Me, all who are weary and heavy-laden," Jesus announced, "and I will give you rest" (Matthew 11:28). Christ is now our Sabbath, not for a 24-hour period once a week, but an everlasting rest we can enjoy moment by moment.

These foods, festivals, tabernacles, temples, and observances were preparatory and transitional, not permanent. These "things that are on earth" are intended to lead us to the Lord Jesus. The nineteenth century English evangelical clergyman Charles Simeon, in his fabulous book about how the persons, institutions, and events in the Old Testament prefigured Christ, expounds:

> The types are of signal use to *us*, in that *they testify of Christ as the person promised* from the foundation of the world, *and prefigured in* the whole of the *Mosaic ritual*. When we compare the account of Christ in the *New* Testament with the various ordinances of the *Old*, we see how impossible it was that such a coincidence of character should ever happen, but by the express ordination and appointment of God. But they are of further use to us also, in that *they wonderfully illustrate the character of Jesus*. We could not have formed any adequate idea of Christ's work and offices, if we had not been assisted by the typical institutions: *these* serve to embody our notions, and to make them, like a picture, visible to the eyes of men, and therefore intelligible to the meanest capacity: whereas, if we could not thus invest them, as it were, with matter, we could only offer to our

hearers some abstract ideas, which, after all, would convey but little meaning, and leave no abiding impression.[19]

These Old Testament pictures are helpful as visual aids to educate us about Christ. So don't throw away the pictures, but see them for what they are. They're pictures, "things that are on earth," that when rightly used can aid us in laying hold of the heavenly, spiritual realities that they represent in Jesus. But if we devote our energy into the earthly, the preparatory, the ABCs, we subtly lose out on the riches in Christ. Legalism, an over-attentiveness to the letter of the law rather than the essence of the law, takes you backwards to the shadows and makes those the reality. "The main point is keeping the Sabbath and following all the rules of the Passover." No, Jesus is the main point. All of these preparatory things serve to etch unforgettable images in our minds that shape our conceptions of Christ's work and offices as prophet, priest, and king.

Seeking the Above
John the Baptist came as the forerunner, the one who ran on ahead to prepare the people for the One to come. John recognized the difference between words originating from heaven above or from earth below. As a burning and shining lamp finishing his predetermined course, the Baptizer declared:

---

[19] Simeon, Charles, *Helps to Composition on Six Hundred Skeletons of Sermons; Several Being the Substance of Sermons Preached Before the University; Vol 2, The Third Edition* (London: Luke Hansard & Sons, 1815), p. 3

He who comes from above is above all, he who is of the earth is from the earth and speaks of the earth. He who comes from heaven is above all (John 3:31).

John spoke in an earthly way. He baptized in an earthly way, that is, in a preparatory way, much as the alphabet prepares one to read and write. John's baptism with its earthly, tangible element (water) was to be superseded by the Son of God's heavenly, intangible baptism in the Holy Spirit. "As for me," John preached, "I baptize you with water; but One is coming who is mightier than I, and I am not fit to untie the thong of His sandals; He will baptize you with the Holy Spirit and fire" (Luke 3:16). The former introduces the latter, which is permanently established by Christ. Paul reverberates along that same line, contrasting Adam and Jesus:

> The first man, Adam, became a living soul. The last Adam became a life-giving spirit. However, the spiritual is not first, but the natural; then the spiritual. The first man is from the earth, earthy; the second man is from heaven (1 Corinthians 15:47).

So back to our original question: What exactly are "the things that are above" that we are to seek and to set our minds on? What ball are we to keep our eye on? Paul does not leave us in the dark about it. Paul's heavenly message, in sharp contrast to these earthly teachings, is that the gospel, Christ and Him crucified, is "the above." So when Paul says to seek the above, he is reiterating his previous warnings to stay true to those like Epaphras "who preached the gospel to you by the Holy Spirit sent from heaven" (1 Peter 1:12). Paul's supreme focus, here as well as every other one of his letters and sermons, is the person and finished work of Jesus Christ.

> Him we proclaim, warning everyone and teaching everyone with all wisdom, that we may present everyone mature in Christ (Colossians 1:28 ESV).

The manner in which Paul proclaimed Christ was either by warning or by teaching.[20] Paul's theme did not deviate from that of the twelve apostles. "And every day, in the temple and from house to house, they kept right on teaching and preaching Jesus as the Christ" (Acts 5:42). Likewise, Paul's gospel has at its heart the Lord Jesus Christ. This is the message, when heard and understood, ushers us to the chain-shattering, sin-emancipating Savior who produces a life of faith and love.

Now when Paul uses the term *gospel*, keep in mind that it is not limited to the New Testament, which was still a work in progress at that time. When the apostles preached the gospel, they proclaimed Jesus Christ from the Old Testament—the books of Moses, the Prophets, and the Psalms. Later on, when Matthew, Mark, Luke, and John compiled their Gospels, they often quoted from the Old Testament in light of Jesus' historical fulfillment. "Then beginning with Moses and with all the prophets, [Jesus] explained to them the things concerning Himself in all the Scriptures" (Luke 24:27). So gospel teaching encompasses any passage from the Bible that unveils the Lord Jesus. Setting our minds on the things above means, then, to welcome the revelation of Christ from Scripture. An indispensable principle of Bible study is total reliance upon

---

[20] "Warning" and "teaching" are present participles that clarify the main verb "proclaim." His proclamation consisted of either warning or teaching.

God's Holy Spirit to show us the Lord Jesus.[21]   That's the *above* we're admonished to set our minds upon.

Where's Christ?

Are you ready for some more exciting news? When we seek the above, the gospel, that's where Christ is!

> If then you have been raised with Christ, *seek the things that are above, where Christ is,* seated at the right hand of God. Set your minds on things that are above, not on things that are on earth (Colossians 3:1-2).

Realize that Paul is speaking in heavenly terms, not of the earth, so don't let the geographical language, "seated at the right hand of God," throw you off. He speaks of things as they are, not as they appear. We have been raised with Christ. Our life is now hid with Christ in God. Hebrews 12:22 says we have already come to Mount Zion, the heavenly Jerusalem of jubilant saints and angels. God "seated us with Him in the heavenly places in Christ Jesus," Ephesians 2:6 says. Though we're not seeing an angel fest or God's throne room right now as we sit in our living room recliner, yet by faith we trust God's truth about the way things really are. So when we seek the above, the Scripture, God's heaven-sent word, that is where we find Christ!

Not only do we find the written word, the gospel, pointing to the living Word, Jesus, but Paul adds, "where Christ is, seated at the right hand of God." Jesus, the Man in glory, seated at God's right hand, communicates several things to us. First, it speaks of abundance. It was when

---

[21] In my study of Scripture, I've assimilated this principle from Ed Miller, who stresses this at the beginning of every one of his teachings.

Christ was exalted to the right hand of God that He lavishly poured out the Holy Spirit (Acts 2:33). Paul affirmed the same openhandedness in Ephesians 4:10: "He who descended is Himself also He who ascended far above all the heavens, so that He might fill all things." We can be confident that as we seek the above, the Scripture which points to Christ, there we will encounter King Jesus in His abundant fullness to meet our every need.

Jesus seated at the right hand of God also communicates completeness. The book of Hebrews points out the priests who always stood, for their work was never completed, but Christ, having completed redemption, having purged our sins, sat down (Hebrews 10:11-12). His seated posture pictures a finished work. So setting your mind on the above specially includes Christ's finished work. You've been forgiven all your transgressions and reconciled to God through the sacrifice of the thorn-crowned King. You've been set free from the prince of darkness, the devil, who was disarmed and rendered powerless through Jesus' triumphal death (Colossians 2:15, Hebrews 2:14). God has rooted you securely in Christ who's finished it all! As you think on these things, discouragement and doubt will diminish.

Earlier we looked at the life of Christ waiting to spring forth from the seed of the word of God. When we occupy our thoughts and affections on the above, the Scripture, the Spirit unveils Christ to us. This aligns with the cornerstone verse: "As you have therefore received Christ Jesus the Lord, so walk in Him." You received Christ by faith, through hearing and understanding the preached word:

> Of this you have heard before in the word of the truth, the gospel, which has come to you, as indeed in the whole world it is bearing fruit and growing—as it also does

among you, since the day you heard it and understood the grace of God in truth (Colossians 1:5-6 ESV).

These Colossians received Christ Jesus the Lord the very day they heard and understood the grace of God, the word of the truth, the gospel. "Bearing fruit and growing" is the evidence that Christ, the hope of glory, is within. As we originally received Christ Himself through setting our minds on the gospel, so we're to continue occupying our thoughts with the gospel, for He is still to be found there. The written Scripture provides abundant opportunities to receive Christ over and over again.

The first time we heard the gospel and trusted in Christ, we received Him in all His fullness. As we continue setting our minds on the gospel, we are not receiving a Christ that we don't already have, but rather receiving of His fullness that is already ours but haven't yet experienced or enjoyed. In the last chapter of this book, we will compare our little by little receiving of Christ to Israel progressively possessing the Promised Land, a picture of Christ in His abundance. Like the progressiveness of the conquests under Joshua, the judges, and the kings to actual possession and enjoyment what God had already fully given to them, so it is with us on a spiritual plane. So our spiritual pilgrimage is not a one-time event, but a continual exploration of the frontiers of Scripture where our guide, the Holy Spirit, freely gives us more of Christ to receive and enjoy. "[The Spirit] will glorify Me," Jesus explained, "for He will take of Mine and will disclose it to you" (John 16:14).

Recall from Colossians chapter 1 the spiritual war being waged against the hope of the gospel. Satanic strategy assaults our confidence in Jesus Christ as being our all in all today. Paul briefed the Corinthians regarding this undermining, demonic strategy:

And even if our gospel is veiled, it is veiled to those who are perishing, in whose case the god of this world has blinded the minds of the unbelieving so that they might not see the light of the gospel of the glory of Christ, who is the image of God (2 Corinthians 4:3-4).

While the context of this passage has immediate relevance to unbelievers, Satan is also busy sidetracking believers away from the light of the gospel of the glory of Christ. Satan fears our focus on the glory of Christ in the gospel and does his best to obscure it with "things that are on earth," these teachings centered in the beginner principles—foods, drinks, festivals, temples, do not handle/taste/touch—that do not terminate in Jesus Christ. So stop dwelling on other messages that take you away from Him. Setting your affections on the Lord Jesus Christ as revealed in God's word is where you'll get life. As we receive Him, so we walk in Him.

Victory over sin and actively representing Christ's character in every relationship in the home, in the church, and in the world progressively advances as you're setting your mind on the above. Impurity is not conquered by doing more and trying harder but by seeing and receiving more of our awesome Christ. Sin has already been conquered by our Conqueror, in whom we are full. When we seek and set our minds on the gospel, the Father reveals His Son to us and applies His past victory on the cross to trump our present indwelling sin. When our lives are free from the domination of sexual immorality, impurity, passion, evil desire, and covetousness, we are appearing with Christ in glory. Christ in us as an unseen hope of glory has bloomed to Christ through us as a visible expression of glory.

So our putting to death the sins of the flesh is

directly dependent upon Christ's appearing—not His second coming but, in total dependence on the Spirit, His continual unveiling from the word of God to the eyes of our heart. Our part of seeking and setting our minds on the above is over-abundantly answered by God's part of revealing this preeminent Jesus to us to put to death the deeds of our flesh.

We breathe because air is readily available. We see because light is immediately accessible. We put to death what is earthly in us because the Father makes the Son preeminent as our life, readily accessible to us. As our head is preeminent to our body, Christ is to His corporate body, the church. As we hold "fast to the Head," from whom all life flows, we grow "with a growth that is from God," Colossians 2:19 says. God has made Christ the power of God unto salvation, a salvation that is past and on-going and one day will be fully consummated when He comes again.

CHAPTER 10

The Might of Christ's Glory

Our Christian life began by coming to the Lord Jesus as a helpless sinner. Yet even after being born again, forgiven, adopted into God's family, and being filled in Christ, we are still helpless. What a glorious day it is when we finally realize that we are absolutely, 100% powerless to change ourselves! God's mighty power, though, does not make up for where we come up short. No, to enjoy victory over the seemingly invincible giant of indwelling sin we need His mighty power to raise us up out of powerlessness—zero strength—to transform us into the image of Jesus Christ.[22]

But what is God's power supply and how do I tap into it? Is it by praying more? Fasting? Reading my Bible or Christian books? Hearing sermons? Going to Christian

---

[22] This section originally appeared in *A More Excellent Way*, "The Mighty Glory of Christ," Winter 2012, Volume 5, Number 1, p. 11 (adapted for use here)

conferences? Listening to praise music? How can I get off the treadmill of the frustration and perpetual discouragement of a defeated Christian life? Understanding this next Colossians principle is a forward step toward maximizing our experience of the power of God.

Paul's answer has to do with showing us the relationship between revelation, receiving Christ, and life, walking in Him. When Paul admonishes us to seek the above, the gospel, there is an organic connection between the revealing of Christ and a growth into His likeness. What God has joined together, let not man separate. A seeking of the above must involve a seeking of light, an unveiling of Christ Jesus the Lord to our hearts through the God-appointed means of His word. But why does the transformation of our character have to involve a revelation of Christ and not some other way?

The Might of His Glory

First of all, we must be convinced by God's word that Christ, the glory of God, is God's power source. Some, citing Romans 1:16, might say, "Isn't the gospel the power of God?" Yes, indeed it is; in particular Paul calls it "the gospel of the glory of Christ" (2 Corinthians 4:4). In Colossians, Paul sheds light on the combining of God's glory and His might: "May you be strengthened with all power, according to his glorious might" (Colossians 1:11 ESV). The phrase *his glorious might* literally says in the Greek, *the might of the glory of him*.[23] Have you ever considered that God's glory has might? Does that sound a little weird to you, as it did

---

[23] The Greek word for *glorious* is *doxa* (DOX-ah), a noun (glory), not a noun-describing adjective (glorious).

me? Perhaps this strangeness influenced the translators to shy away from the literal rendering, "the might of His glory." Yet Paul did not shrink back from proclaiming this wonderful truth.

In the resurrection of Jesus, God's power and glory are united: "Christ was raised from the dead by the glory of the Father" (Romans 6:4 ESV). The glory that raised Jesus from the dead was no low wattage nightlight glowing on Jesus' body in the tomb. In Ephesians, Paul calls attention to "the working of the strength of His might which He brought about in Christ, when He raised Him from the dead" (Ephesians 1:19-20). So Paul asserts that the resurrection of Christ was caused by the glory of the Father *and* by the working of His great might, "the immeasurable greatness of His power"! There is much mystery here, but no contradiction, for the Lord Jesus Christ was raised by the Father's glory *and* power. The Father's glory *is* the manifestation of His mighty power! These are beautifully intertwined in the phrase "the might of His glory."

As God fashioned our physical world to communicate spiritual realities, the sun as the light of the world ultimately pictures Jesus Christ, "the true Light which gives light to every man coming into the world" (John 1:9 NKJV). Light is a metaphor for glory. For example, the light of the sun *is* its glory, for those rays reveal the sun's grandeur to us. This glory has incredible might! According to my Internet "wiki" sources and calculator skills, every *hour* the glory of the sun lifts up into rainclouds about 350 trillion pounds of water— the estimated weight of Mount Everest, the world's highest mountain! Our physical world testifies that glory has might!

Life and Light Revealed
In the Bible there is a close bond between light and life.

From the very beginning, the voice of God decreed, "Let there be light," and life quickly followed after. Light and life in the plant world abundantly testify to this truth. The glory of the sun is what makes all life on the earth possible. Through the process of photosynthesis, the leaves of plants are specially designed to convert the sun's rays (i.e., solar energy) into consumable food. The light becomes life-sustaining energy, or might, for the plant. The light is its life. Take away the light and the plant dies. Life and light are interwoven for humanity also, as John 1:4 attests, "In Him was life, and the life was the Light of men."

John goes on to instruct us how this Light, an open display of the hidden God, was an uncovering of His glory.

> And the Word became flesh, and dwelt among us, and we saw His glory, glory as of the only begotten from the Father, full of grace and truth....For of His fullness we have all received, and grace upon grace (John 1:14, 16).

Notice how "For of His fullness we have all received, and grace upon grace" follows "we saw His glory." After the Word became flesh, the *life* of Christ (His fullness, grace upon grace) conveys to mankind through the *light* of Christ (His glory, the revelation of Him). John and Paul are in agreement that "of His fullness we have all received," for Paul, as we have examined, enlarged this, saying, "For in him the whole fullness of deity dwells bodily, and you have been filled in him" (Colossians 2:9-10 ESV). This fullness happened, Paul wrote in the letter, when we received Christ through hearing and understanding the word of truth, a knowledge that Scripture routinely calls light. So the life of fullness is the direct result of receiving the light, or glory, of Jesus, the eternal Word.

The knowledge of the glory of God is called *Light*

here in this parallel between nature's creation and the new creation in the heart of man:

> For God, who said, "Light shall shine out of darkness," is the One who has shone in our hearts to give the Light of the knowledge of the glory of God in the face of Christ (2 Corinthians 4:6).

The revealed knowledge of Christ (i.e., light) is directly associated with the Christian life. So when Christ, the Light of men, appears in glory and shines in our hearts, that's when spiritual life flourishes in us, even more so than our lush, green earth does when bathing in the sunshine.

Jesus as our Immanuel, God with us, had the unsurpassable advantage that no other prophet or divine representative in the Old Testament ever had: to shine the unsullied, unobstructed glory of God, in our hearts.

> Long ago, at many times and in many ways, God spoke to our fathers by the prophets, but in these last days he has spoken to us by his Son…. He is the radiance of the glory of God and the exact imprint of his nature (Hebrews 1:1-3).

The Lord Jesus affirmed this principle of seeing Him, the radiance of the glory of God, and receiving life:

> For this is the will of my Father, that *everyone who looks on [theōreō] the Son and believes in him should have eternal life*, and I will raise him up on the last day (John 6:40 ESV).

Greek has a dozen words translated into our simple word "look" or "see." Each has subtle nuances that vary from a casual observation to an intense, studied concentration. *Theōreō* (THAY-oh-RAY-oh) for *looks on* is a careful scrutinizing, the kind of critical inspection that the general of the army would have of his soldiers in a parade, not the easygoing onlooker among the spectators. Like the disciples who strained their eyes to catch the last glimpses of the Lord Jesus as He ascended upwards towards heaven, it is this kind of mesmerizing, captivated heart-looking to Christ that the Father wills to unite with eternal life.

Tapping Into God's Mighty Power

The glory of Jesus Christ is God's mighty power. For many years I thought tapping into God's power was through spiritual disciplines like fasting, prayer, and getting up really early to read the Bible. I talked earlier about how Bible study without God's tools is like giving a starving man a can of beans without a can opener. It's quite possible to touch the outside of spiritual disciplines without ever quite reaching God's heart. So how do we experience the might of God's glory?

When Paul, as Saul of Tarsus, a vicious persecutor of the fledgling Christian church, encountered Jesus on the road to Damascus, that glory transformed him. What happened in dramatic fashion there and then is loaded with spiritual principles for our transformation from glory to glory here and now. From 2 Corinthians 3 comes Paul's most precise lesson on how Christians should study their Bibles:

> For to this day, when they read the old covenant, that same veil remains unlifted, because only through Christ is it taken away. Yes, to this day whenever Moses is read a veil lies over their hearts. But when one turns to the Lord, the veil is removed. Now the Lord is the Spirit, and where the Spirit of the Lord is, there is freedom. And we all,

with unveiled face, beholding the glory of the Lord, are being transformed into the same image from one degree of glory to another. For this comes from the Lord who is the Spirit (2 Corinthians 3:14-18 ESV).

So when we turn toward the Lord "who is the Spirit,"[24] He lifts the veil over our minds and our Bible to show us the transforming glory of Jesus Christ! This "glory of the Lord" that we, with unveiled face, all behold is "the glory of God in the face of Jesus Christ" (2 Corinthians 4:6). So our conformity to the image of Jesus is molded by the Spirit of God repeatedly lifting the veil off the Bible to show us the glory of Jesus. As our body requires us to eat every day, so our spirit, our "new self," needs a continual series of "comings" of Christ to energize its transformation from glory to glory. When we orient our hearts to the Spirit of the Lord, He opens our minds and hearts to see Jesus Christ in His word as He truly is and then transforms us into that same image. "As we gaze on Jesus, as we behold his goodness, his glory, we are changed into his likeness, the most beautiful Person of all."[25]

When Jesus Christ steps down from His heavenly throne to return to earth, that coming will be an open revelation of glory to mankind as the Light of the world. Every eye will see His full radiance, even those who pierced Him (Revelation 1:7). So while our appearing with the Lord Jesus Christ in glory is a breathtaking truth when He comes again, let's not miss the magnitude of His daily comings now. Though we will fully become like our Lord and Savior Jesus

---

[24] This is an extremely rare occurrence where *Lord* refers to the Holy Spirit, not Jesus Christ. "Now the Lord is the Spirit..."

[25] Eldridge, John & Stasi, *Captivating: Unveiling the Mystery of a Woman's Soul* (Nashville: Thomas Nelson, 2005) p. 146

Christ when He comes again (1 John 3:2), we are also progressively changed from glory to glory now, as we captivatingly look for Christ with the eyes of the heart, anticipating His glory from the word of God. As we heed Paul's admonition to seek the above, the Scripture, the Spirit then unveils the glory of Jesus, swapping our powerlessness with His might to enable us to walk in the newness of life!

So should we pray? Yes, but purposing to see the glory of Jesus Christ. Should we read our Bibles? Yes, but with a heart confidently dependent upon the Spirit to unveil to our hearts the exceeding riches of the glory of Jesus Christ. Then as the Spirit reveals the Christ of glory to us, we will abound in the riches of walking in the newness of life!

In prayer Paul plugged the kitchen appliances of "all endurance and patience with joy" into the outlet of the might of His glory.

> May you be strengthened with all power, according to his glorious might, for all endurance and patience with joy (Colossians 1:11 ESV).

The applications of Christ's mighty glory to our daily lives far exceed joyful patience and endurance, as wonderful as those are. The broader principle is more easily observed in Romans 6. The chapter begins with a question, "Shall we continue in sin that grace may abound?" Paul exclaims, "By no means!" His answer revolves around the might of His glory.

> Therefore we have been buried with Him through baptism into death, so that as Christ was raised from the dead through the glory of the Father, so we too might walk in newness of life (Romans 6:4).

Our union with Christ in His death includes our union in His resurrection. So the means of getting more grace after we've been united to Christ is not by sinning more (or trying harder to be good!). We receive grace and power to walk in the newness of life—to live the Christian life—by receiving the glory of God, a glory brimming over with might. We as believers do have a part to play, spotlighted here in Colossians as getting into the "Sonshine." As you have received Christ Jesus the Lord—the Light of the world, beaming glory into our hearts—so walk in Him.

Part 3

Practical Steps for Preeminently Jesus Daily Living

CHAPTER 11

Christ's Preeminence in Character

In Part 1, "Diagnosing Doubt and Discouragement: Amnesia in a Jesus Universe," Paul put his finger on the root problem plaguing this vigorous faith community in Colossae: discouragement. Their discouragement over the sins popping up in their lives made them susceptible to these new faddish teachers in town through whom the kingdom of darkness was secretly at work to shift and shake them off their hope of the gospel. This satanic assault did not aim at getting them to desert Jesus Christ outright, but to subtly undermine their view of Him as a present, preeminent deliverer from their flesh. This crafty strategy gradually and imperceptibly warped their faith in the real Jesus they'd learned through the gospel to a different, less than preeminent Jesus.

Paul reminded this discouraged bunch how the gospel preached by their evangelist, Epaphras, was what introduced them to Christ Himself. When they received Christ, it was *He* who eradicated the scum of all their nature and beautified their lives with love. They had to relearn, or perhaps discover for the first time, that they were surrounded on all sides—in the heavens and all the earth—by a preeminent, all-surpassing Jesus. The cure for their discouragement, and ours, is when the unrivaled, undiminished object of trust is preeminently Jesus.

In Part 2, "The Glorious Riches of Christ's Fullness is Power for Holiness Today," we saw that God divulged to Paul His ancient secret—Christ dwelling within all classes of mankind, Jew and Gentile. This open secret unlocks the door to experiencing the fantastic wealth of the fullness of Christ. The aged apostle handpicked for his divine scrapbook some snapshots of this colossal Christ—Creator, Savior, Redeemer, soil, fruit, fullness, circumciser, substitute, victor, head, and others. He invites us to relax, sit back, and enjoy *this* Christ whom we've received. Regardless of our dismal, lackluster spiritual performance, we are full in Christ, in whom dwells all the fullness of the Trinity. By contrast, the false teachers in Colossae majored in the preparatory principles, the ABCs, that were worthless in curbing the indulgence of the flesh. There's no formula or program outside of Jesus to revive our weary, discouraged souls. Everything we need to walk in a manner worthy of our high calling is in Him.

If we miss this point in Colossians, we can find our spiritual journey not unlike Lightning McQueen, spinning our wheels with great energy but with little forward progress. If we're ever to see victory over these ever-present fleshly habits and sinful tendencies, Christ has to come. It's His life that defeats the activities of indwelling sin. Paul warned that if it's not the life of Jesus, if it's not holding fast to the Head, or if it's not receiving His fullness, it has "no value against fleshly indulgence" (Colossians 2:23). These other new fangled messages may appear wise, profitable, and results-oriented, but their underlying core principles are

Eden's tree of the knowledge of good and evil, falsely promising to make one wise and be like God. Eating from their tree brings death. Partaking of the one Tree of life, Christ, is our one solution.

That's why Paul beats one drum about a preeminent Christ. His whole letter is in sync with its rhythm. Even verses that seem to deviate, like an allusion to the second coming ("When Christ, who is our life, is revealed, then you also will be revealed with Him in glory"), march in step to a preeminent Christ who calls us to walk in Him. The glory of Christ, God's power plant, puts to death what's earthly in us and radiates out of us a heavenly life of love toward God and man. Paul's prayer, "May you be strengthened with all power, according to his glorious might" (Colossians 1:11 ESV), is literally *the might of his glory*. So Christ's glory shines in our hearts to power up our spiritual life far greater than even the light of the sun that empowers all life on our lush, green earth. As He has made sunshine universally accessible to us, the Father delights to make His Son preeminent as our life.

Back in Chapter 9 "Seeking the Above" we showed how, in sharp contrast to these earthly teachings, Paul's heavenly message—the gospel teaching of Christ and Him crucified—is "the above." The gospel—any passage of the Bible that unveils the Lord Jesus—is the ball we're to keep our eye on, not "things that are on earth," those philosophies or doctrines steeped in human tradition and effort or the preparatory, shadowy precepts of the Old Testament (e.g., food and drink prohibitions) that find their permanent, spiritual reality in Christ Jesus. So when we seek the above, the gospel, that's where we find Christ Himself in His abundance and completeness. When we absorb our minds with the above, with a captivated heart-looking to Christ, eternal life flourishes. Tapping into God's power is not by aimlessly packing our schedules with prayer, fasting, the Bible, books, sermons, music, seminars, conferences, service, and evangelism. While we do involve ourselves in these, our laser focus needs to be where God puts it. Our spiritual transformation happens when the Holy Spirit repeatedly takes away the veil from the word of God to show us the might-filled glory of Jesus (2 Corinthians 3:15-18). So we're to relish continual comings of Christ in the midst of Christian activities and spiritual disciplines.

In Part 3, "Practical Steps for Preeminently Jesus Daily Living," we explore what experiencing a preeminent Christ really looks like in daily life and practice. Now, Paul is not satisfied with lofty talk about a universe-surpassing Jesus without connecting the dots to how that influences how we live here and now. So Colossians 3 fleshes out the glory of Christ in general principles—putting sin to death, putting on Christ our life, and transforming our personal relationships. This chapter develops what the preeminence of Jesus Christ looks like in the daily grind—replying to emails in your office cubicle, cooking noodles in the kitchen, playing with Legos with your kids on the floor, hanging out with people from church, or coexisting with other motorists on the road. Colossians 4 showcases more snapshots of grace, preeminence made public in ordinary folks like Tychicus and Epaphras who encountered and held fast to an extraordinary, all-sufficient Jesus. So if I've embraced Christ preeminent as He should be to me, what should my day-to-day life look like?

Preeminence: Christ Is All
The preeminence of Jesus Christ appeared very quickly in Paul's letter. As Creator of everything in the universe,

visible and invisible, Christ is preeminent, above all. Without Him this universe would blow apart, for "in Him all things hold together" (Colossians 1:17)! As God has made Jesus Christ preeminent in the created universe, how much more He intends to do so in the church. The widespread life of Jesus is already appearing throughout the church, in the individual members of His body:

> But we have this treasure in jars of clay, to show that the surpassing power belongs to God and not to us. We are afflicted in every way...always carrying in the body the death of Jesus, so that the life of Jesus may also be manifested in our bodies (2 Corinthians 4:7-8, 10 ESV).

As we get into the practical sections in the latter half of the letter, Paul hasn't dropped his earlier theme about Christ being preeminent. This monumental arch in chapter 1 spans into chapters 3 and 4. As chapter 3 opens, it is not us appearing center stage with Jesus as best supporting actor standing close by, but the other way around.

> For you have died, and your life is hidden with Christ in God. When Christ who is your life appears, then you also will appear with him in glory (Colossians 3:3 ESV).

Jesus, the preeminent one perennially having the first place, appears, and then we with Him. What a grand statement about Jesus Christ being preeminent! The glory only appears to be ours because it is our face that wears it, but it is really Christ in us, the hope of glory, shining through.

Furthermore, Paul's earlier note about the universal effectiveness of the gospel is picked up again in chapter 3. The fruit-bearing result of the gospel transcends the diversities of races, nations, peoples, and tongues.

> Of which you previously heard in the word of truth, the gospel which has come to you, just as in all the world also it is constantly bearing fruit and increasing, even as it has been doing in you also since the day you heard of it and understood the grace of God in truth (Colossians 1:5-6).

So the white light of "bearing fruit" in chapter 1 is split out like a prism into its distinct rainbow hues in chapter 3:

> Here there is not Greek and Jew, circumcised and uncircumcised, barbarian, Scythian, slave, free; but Christ is all, and in all. *Put on then, as God's chosen ones, holy and beloved, compassionate hearts, kindness, humility, meekness, and patience, bearing with one another* and, if one has a complaint against another, *forgiving each other*; as the Lord has forgiven you, so you also must forgive (Colossians 3:11-13 ESV).

The colorful menagerie of Christian virtues—heart of compassion, kindness, humility, meekness, patience, forgiveness, love—is what was meant earlier by *bearing fruit*. Paul attributes this to *Christ is all, and in all*. That's just another way of saying preeminence. He's everything! Since Christ's preeminence is wholly transcendent of time, people, and place, Paul argues, we can expect the same fruitfulness right now.

Paul provides a number of indicators that Jesus' preeminence is at work in our character:

> But now you also, put them all aside: anger, wrath, malice, slander, and abusive speech from your mouth. Do

not lie to one another, since you laid aside the old self with its evil practices, and have put on the new self who is being renewed to a true knowledge according to the image of the One who created him (Colossians 3:8-10).

Putting off the old self and putting on the new self are all expressions of the life of Jesus, our appearing with Him in glory. Putting away anger, gossip, and mean-spirited speech are proofs that the preeminence of Jesus is at work in our lives. His dominion affects our responses on social media, the blogosphere, and comments to articles on the worldwide web. Abusive speech is commonplace on the Internet where anonymity emboldens barbed wire words one would never say in face-to-face conversation. A mark of Christ's supremacy is putting away this slander and abusive, caustic speech, whether in cyberspace or with our next door neighbor. Jesus' preeminence is not some intangible how-many-angels-can-dance-on-the-head-of-a-pin type theological mumbo jumbo disconnected from daily living. Jesus, who is preeminent in everything else, wants to be preeminent in everything concrete and meaningful in our day-to-day lives.

A Stupendous Conclusion

Because *Christ is all, and in all*, Paul makes a stupendous conclusion:

> But Christ is all, and in all. Put on then, as God's chosen ones, holy and beloved, compassionate hearts, kindness, humility, meekness, and patience (Colossians 3:11-12 ESV).

The only reason any of us can have *compassionate*

hearts is because Christ is all (*He* is our compassion) and *in all* of us, regardless of religious, cultural or gender differences. Every Christian has the complete inheritance in Christ. The Greek word for *then* in "Put on then" is *oun* (OON), a word often used in logic and argument for *therefore.* The colorful parade of Christian virtues—compassionate hearts, kindness, humility, meekness, patience, forgiveness, love—has a definite connection to what precedes it: *Christ is all, and in all.* Because Christ *is* all and He's *in* all, because of *this* fact, we can put on all these winsome character traits, or as Paul says in Romans, "Put on Christ."

> Let us walk properly, as in the day, not in revelry and drunkenness, not in lewdness and lust, not in strife and envy. But put on the Lord Jesus Christ, and make no provision for the flesh, to fulfill its lusts (Romans 13:13-14 NKJV).

While entire sermons elaborating on each of these virtues in Colossians 3 can be helpful, Paul is just giving a sampling here, not a comprehensive list. The fruit of the Spirit—love, joy, peace, patience, kindness, goodness, faithfulness, gentleness, self-control—and every other spiritually attractive character quality from Genesis to Revelation is included, because these are all the manifestations of Jesus Christ in us.

Any time we truly act as Christians in love, what's happening? When these characteristics manifest in Christians, this is "the life of Jesus [being] manifested in our bodies" (2 Corinthians 4:10 ESV). Or to phrase it as Paul did in Colossians, this is appearing with Christ in glory! The exhibition of love is not because we're keeping a set of rules or putting our flesh under a rigorous regimen. You know, we get up at 3 a.m. every day to pray, and fast ten times a week. Can some of these things be beneficial? They can, but the main point that Paul is stressing here is Jesus' preeminence. It stems back to "Whenever Christ, who is our life, appears, you also will appear with Him in glory" (Colossians 3:4). We have considered the cause and effect relationship between glory and might, light and life. Every time the Spirit unveils Jesus from the above, the gospel, along with that glory comes His immeasurably great power to raise us up out of the barrenness of our flesh into a heavenly, fruitful life. The might of Christ's glory has a divine energy far superior to sunshine that lifts a Mount Everest of water into the sky every hour. So any compassion, humility, love, or joy in our life is because Christ, the hope of glory, is being manifested now. This is what Christ looks like now in glory!

Glory is not one of God's many attributes, such as holiness, love, or justice. Glory is all of His attributes combined; it's who He is. Any time we "put on" a compassionate heart, that's a glimpse of who this compassionate God is. Our joyfulness in the midst of trying circumstances is the glory, the outshining, or the radiance of who our joyful Sovereign is. Although the Lord Jesus is disguised, as it were, among the individual members of His body, the church, people are actually seeing Him, but in a spiritual sense. Paul learned this lesson on the very first day of his conversion, which Luke, the beloved physician, chronicled in Acts:

> He fell to the ground and heard a voice saying to him, "Saul, Saul, why are you persecuting Me?" And he said, "Who are You, Lord?" And He said, "I am Jesus whom you are persecuting" (Acts 9:4-5).

When Saul was assisting those who stoned Stephen, and dragging men and women off to prison, little did he know that behind all of these Christians stood Christ the Lord. So any time others see love or kindness or joy displayed in our lives, it is Jesus! That's the preeminence of Christ in our personality and character.

CHAPTER 12
Entering the Beautiful Gate

Every time the Father reveals Christ, He is revealing Him in such a way that He is our holiness. Christ is our love; Christ is our kindness; Christ is our humility. That's what Paul is saying to us in Colossians by stating that when Christ our life appears, you will appear with Him in glory. That's preeminence, and it's expressed by our putting on love. The invisible Lord is being revealed through our visible presence on earth. Any time we "put on love, which is the perfect bond of unity" (Colossians 3:14), *Christ* is that love. God in Christ performs this. We're just clay vessels through which the excellent Treasure is shining. Therefore, be seeking to know Jesus. Be seeking the above, the word of God, where you'll see Him and receive Him. As you do, He'll manifest in these ways so that everything else about your spiritual life will fall into place.

Now, Christ being our holiness may seem strange in our society where the commonly accepted norm is to credit good deeds and behavior to the person. Yet Scripture gives ample testimony that this is so. For example, Paul says to the Corinthian believers:

But by His doing you are in Christ Jesus, *who became to us* wisdom from God, and righteousness and *sanctification*, and redemption, so that, just as it is written, "Let him who boasts, boast in the Lord" (1 Corinthians 1:30-31).

Jesus Christ became to us sanctification? Sanctification is a rare word you don't hear in the conversations of the world today. Sanctification, or holiness, simply means being set apart to God in thought, word, and deed. The life of our Lord Jesus displayed in the Gospels—Matthew, Mark, Luke, and John—is what sanctification ultimately is. God sees us forgiven of every sin and already perfect in Jesus Christ (justification). In sanctification the world sees us more and more like Jesus Christ in our character (well, because it is Jesus!).

So Jesus Christ is made unto us sanctification, our character that showcases the new creation. This is a marvelous truth! God the Father has made our Lord Jesus Christ our sanctification, our holiness, *just as* He was made our righteousness. Do you worship your holiness? You should! Because, according to Scripture, your holiness is Jesus Christ Himself. Therefore, as Paul writes, how can *we* boast? We do not manufacture righteousness or fabricate our own holiness. Our boast of these evidences of grace is a boast in the Lord, because it *is* the Lord. "Let your light shine before men in such a way that they may see your good works, and glorify your Father who is in heaven" (Matthew 5:16). The Father, not us, gets the glory for our good works because He is the one who made Jesus unto us our shining holiness.

To illustrate this point within Colossians, when Paul prays about their love for all the saints, notice how he doesn't thank *them* for it.

We always thank *God, the Father of our Lord Jesus Christ,* when we pray for you, since we heard of your faith in Christ Jesus and of the love that you have for all the saints (Colossians 1:3-4 ESV).

Paul never thanks believers in this epistle (or nearly all of his other epistles) for their love.[26] He directs the thanksgiving for their love towards God because *He* is the source of it. This all-pervasive love among the saints is God's manifestation of Christ as the firstborn from the dead that "in everything he might be preeminent" (Colossians 1:18 ESV).

We who have been united to Christ in His death experience a union with Him in His resurrection glory. Jesus holds everything together in the universe by the word of His power. Jesus holds everything together in our spiritual lives, too, exercising His kingly authority by putting all enemies like sin under His feet. We don't see these things with our natural eyes, but faith trusts what God has revealed in His immutable word. May God give us spiritual eyes to see it in ourselves and others to the effect of much joy, thankfulness, and praise to our great Savior!

Jesus Christ Takes Us Through the Beautiful Gate

Every time we manifest the love of Christ, this is Christ, who is our life, appearing in glory. "Well, I don't feel Jesus." Let us lay aside our subjective feelings and trust what God says

---

[26] Romans 16:3-4 is the only reference of Paul thanking any believers directly: "Greet Prisca and Aquila, my fellow workers in Christ Jesus, who for my life risked their own necks, to whom not only do I give thanks, but also all the churches of the Gentiles."

in His word. Let's examine a passage where this spiritual reality is more clearly illustrated. In Acts 3 Peter extended his hand to a lame beggar at the Beautiful Gate of the temple. The crowds who saw the miraculous healing naturally attributed it to him. Since Peter couldn't take the credit, he corrected their misconceptions.

> Men of Israel, why do you wonder at this, or why do you stare at us, as though by our own power or piety we have made him walk? The God of Abraham, the God of Isaac, and the God of Jacob, the God of our fathers, glorified his servant Jesus (Acts 3:12-13 ESV).

God the Father openly glorified the hidden life of His servant Jesus. Peter didn't have special powers that made the cripple walk. The hand of this Galilean fisherman revealed the unseen heavenly hand of Christ, who strengthened the useless legs of the lame man. So what *appeared as* Peter healing the lame man was really Jesus Christ healing him. Christ, who was hidden in heaven, displayed Himself on earth through Peter. To use the language of Colossians 3, when God manifested Jesus Christ, Peter appeared with Him in glory. The invisible Jesus, not Peter, was the preeminent one in this public display of God's glory. God made His servant, Jesus, conspicuous.

What the Lord Jesus began to do and teach, He continues, but now through His body, the church (Acts 1:1). This Jesus who walked the streets of Palestine, the shores of the Sea of Galilee, and the temple courts of Jerusalem is the same Jesus doing and teaching through Christians everywhere today. Though we can't see Him, He is actively manifesting Himself. Paul elsewhere affirmed this fact:

> For I will not venture to speak of anything except what

Christ has accomplished through me to bring the Gentiles to obedience—by word and deed (Romans 15:18 ESV).

Though Paul was involved in planting churches, Christ was *the* Church Planter, doing and teaching through him. Paul lived an exchanged life[27]—Christ's life in place of his life:

> I have been crucified with Christ. It is no longer I who live, but Christ who lives in me. And the life I now live in the flesh I live by faith in the Son of God, who loved me and gave himself for me (Galatians 2:20 ESV).

So when Paul encourages his readers to seek the things above so that Christ's preeminence would express itself in their daily living, he is speaking from personal experience. These are not untested theories but truth forged in his life through the fires of affliction and trial on this earth. The life he lived in the flesh was Christ living through him. Or as Colossians puts it, God was revealing Jesus Christ, his hidden life, and Paul appeared with Him in glory. Paul lived like Jesus Christ because it was Jesus Christ living. So it is to be with us.

The lame man at the Beautiful Gate points to more than just a physical miracle. The lame man's story is our story. We, too, are handicapped from birth, crippled by sin. We are unable to walk in a manner worthy of God, just as that lame man could not walk in and out of the Beautiful Gate apart from a miracle. The Lord Jesus Christ appears in glory to make the spiritually lame—crippled by sexual immorality, impurity, passion, evil desire, covetousness and

---

[27] The "exchanged life" is a phrase first coined by, Hudson Taylor, the famous English missionary to the Chinese.

other sins of the flesh—to walk through the Beautiful Gate, the perfect soundness of eternal life in Christ. God's command to rise and walk is no less supernatural than any other commandment, for no man can do them without Christ (see John 15:5). "Husbands, love your wives *as Christ...*" "Forgive one another *as Christ.*" "Therefore be perfect *even as your Father is perfect.*" With man these are impossible, but all things are possible with God! So Jesus Christ takes us through the Beautiful Gate, renewing the marred and defaced image of God—the image of Adam—"to a true knowledge according to the image of the One who created him" (Colossians 3:10).

So we can rejoice when we observe the love of God in His people, for what we are seeing is the Father revealing His Son. These are not larger than life people with special holiness powers or the lucky recipients of a genetic jackpot of patience and love ingrained in their DNA. The manifestation of love is the Father making Christ as preeminent in His body, the church, as He is in the created universe.

The corruption of sin has an insatiable habit of distorting our perception of other people. So not only do we need to be quicker to acknowledge Christ as the good in fellow believers, but our perception of their bad needs to be adjusted as well. Even among the problem-riddled Corinthians, Paul had a loving eye towards the grace of God he observed among them.

> I thank my God always concerning you for the grace of God which was given you in Christ Jesus, that in everything you were enriched in Him, in all speech and all knowledge, even as the testimony concerning Christ was confirmed in you, so that you are not lacking in any gift (1 Corinthians 1:4-7).

Bible teacher Zac Poonen impressed me years ago with an illustration that drives home this point:

> I remember hearing a story of a teacher who spread a large white sheet of paper with a small black dot in one corner, in front of his class of students once. He then asked the students what they saw. All of them said that they saw a small black dot in one corner. No one said that they saw the large white sheet. That is how human nature is—blind to the good that there is in others. We only see their black dots.[28]

One evidence that we are experiencing the preeminence of Christ is that we are increasingly perceiving and rejoicing in the white sheet of God's grace in others and less critical of the black spot of their unfinished areas of sanctification. Thanking God diverts our attention from the blemishes to God's amazing manifestation of His Son—the fruit of the Spirit in them. We don't turn a blind eye toward sin, but rather first turn open eyes of faith to the Lord Jesus manifesting Himself. Thankfulness is not something we grit our teeth and try harder at. Rather, if we seek the above as Paul did, receiving the Lord Jesus who ever lives to intercede, we will likewise be thankful intercessors.

Jesus Christ Leads Us to the Mount of Transfiguration
While Jesus walked on earth, Peter was one of the privileged trio that accompanied Him on the Mount of Transfiguration.

---

[28] Poonen, Zac, *The Full Gospel* (Retrieved from http://www.cfcindia.com/web/mainpages/book_window.php?book=the_full _gospel)

After so many scenes where Jesus' appearance was no different from any other Jewish guy's, the radiant glory of God in His face is startling. After Peter awoke, he witnessed the Lord conversing with Moses and Elijah. How cool is that! Notice how Jesus is preeminent here and how glory is ascribed solely to Him:

> Now Peter and his companions had been overcome with sleep; but when they were fully awake, *they saw His glory and the two men standing with Him* (Luke 9:32).

Note that Luke does not draw attention to Moses and Elijah having glory; the glory—*His glory*—is exclusively applied to the Lord Jesus. Christ's is the radiant glory where all human glory fades away and disappears completely. Moses and Elijah were bathed in the glory of the sovereign Lord much like the shepherds on the Bethlehem hillside shone with the glory of the Angel of the Lord. Moses and Elijah had no glory of their own; it was bestowed from Jesus Christ. So it is with every believer lest any man should boast.

Like Moses and Elijah, our glory is not a glory of our own but an out-raying, a shining forth, of Jesus Christ's radiance through us as clay vessels. The glory of God in Christ put on display now in radically transformed character is Jesus Christ manifesting His preeminence in all things. We won't see halos over our heads or faces shining like angels but the fruit of the Spirit that Paul showcases in the rest of chapters 3 and 4. The glory is fathers not provoking their children and children obeying their parents in all things (3:21). The glory is wives submitting to their own husbands and servants working as for the Lord (3:18, 22-24). The glory is prayer and evangelism (4:2-4). This is Christ as firstborn from the dead becoming "in all things Himself the one who is preeminent." The glory is Christ, who is the life, coursing and pulsating through His people moment by moment with the same never-ceasing faithfulness with which He maintains every star, planet, and comet in perfect synchronicity in the universe.

CHAPTER 13

Christ's Preeminence in Society

Charles J. Rolls, in his excellent book, *The Indescribable Christ*, extols the innumerable names and titles of Jesus Christ, one of which is "The All, and In All":

> The title stands at the climax of a forceful summing up in the Colossian Epistle of the famous portrayal of Christ which is made by a twelvefold use of the word "all" in reference to His superior greatness.   The description depicts one of the most complete pictures of His superabounding eminence found in the Scriptures. After declaring that Christ is the Creator of *all* things, Firstborn of *all*, in precedency of *all*, in the pre-eminence of *all*, the Fullness of *all*, the Reconciler of *all*, the Treasury of *all* wisdom, Head of *all* principality, Nourisher of *all* the body, Forgiver of *all* trespasses and such like, the Spirit gives us this choice compendium, "Christ *all*, and in *all*." In God's revealed purpose is a new order of things, in relation to which the division and distinctions of this old creation are of no account.[29]

---

[29] Rolls, Charles J., *The Indescribable Christ: Names and Titles of Jesus Christ A - G* (Neptune, New Jersey: Loizeaux Brothers, 1983), p. 32

In the new order of things, the church, *Christ is all*, that is, He expresses Himself preeminently in all fruit of the Spirit and all spiritual virtues from Genesis to Revelation. Jesus is God's everything; Christ is all. *Christ is in all*, that is, He is within every regenerated child of God, regardless of race, nationality, gender, church denomination, or economic status. Yes, God does distribute different measures of faith in the variety of gifts operating in His body (Romans 12:3-6). But all His children have equal access to Christ for personally manifesting the commonly shared character traits, especially love, the greatest of all.

Jesus is equally available to all God's elect; no one is excluded because he was born a Jew, a Greek, or even the worst of mankind, like a barbarian or Scythian. "For He Himself is our peace, who made both groups [Jew and Gentile] into one and broke down the barrier of the dividing wall" (Ephesians 2:14). In some amusement parks my family has visited, one can purchase a "fast pass," a special privilege of bypassing the long lines to get to the front near the ride. Being raised in a Christian family (a "Jew") does not give one fast pass access to Jesus over the non-churched family (a "Greek"). Human distinctions like race or religion—divisions and distinctions of the old creation—are meaningless when it comes to enjoying Christ and manifesting Him to others. No man-made distinction the world has ever erected has any advantage over any believer who has Christ Himself as a rich inheritance. He is equally gracious and rich in love, joy, peace, and so on to all who call on Him.

Had Paul lived in our day, he might have written, "There is neither Baptist nor Pentecostal, Fundamentalist nor Charismatic, Calvinist nor Arminian, mainline or missional; but Christ is all, and in all." Radical? Yes, but

Christ Himself—and nothing or no one else—is supposed to define us. Nothing man-made should ever usurp the exalted place Jesus should have as the identity of God's people. Divisions exist because we are living in a fallen world; indwelling sin causes God's people to forget who we are in Christ. These man-made distinctions that presume superiority over others in Christ's body are the lies Paul is trying to dismantle.

The good news is that as we seek the above, the word of God, our identity will be more tightly bound up with Jesus Christ and less tethered to man's elitist distinctions like culture, language, religious background, doctrinal position, or denomination. In heaven all of God's people will wave the same palm branch, dress in the same blood-washed white robe, and sing the same song, "Salvation belongs to our God and to the Lamb!" May we as His church on earth increasingly identify with Jesus alone according to this heavenly vision!

Personally Preeminent
Now that Paul has addressed what it means for Christ to be preeminent in general ways in our character—compassion, gentleness, forgiveness, love—he gets a little more personal. Now he'll help us to understand how preeminence works in our commonplace, interpersonal relationships.

> Wives, submit to your own husbands, as is fitting in the Lord. Husbands, love your wives and do not be bitter toward them. Children, obey your parents in all things, for this is well pleasing to the Lord. Fathers, do not provoke your children, lest they become discouraged. Bondservants, obey in all things your masters according to the flesh, not with eyeservice, as men-pleasers, but in

sincerity of heart, fearing God (Colossians 3:18-22 NKJV).

"Wives, submit to your own husbands, as is fitting in the Lord." Is Paul now changing the topic and saying, "Okay, wives, now here's your checklist of what you're supposed to do"? No, he's just using this command to illustrate what "Christ is all, and in all" looks like in everyday life. How does a wife know she's receiving Christ and His fullness described in Colossians 1 and 2? She submits to her own husband, as is fitting in the Lord. That's the test. Submission to her husband is the life of Jesus, the preeminence of Christ, being manifested in the wife. Jesus exhibits His preeminence by living that submissive life through her as she submits to Him.

The all-inclusive scope of Jesus' preeminence can be summed up as, "He is the beginning, the firstborn from the dead, that in everything he might be preeminent" (Colossians 1:18 ESV). Notice how each significant command for holy living in chapter 3 is immediately prefaced with a reference to Jesus becoming preeminent in everything. "Put to death therefore what is earthly in you" follows "When Christ who is your life appears, then you also will appear with him in glory" (Colossians 3:4-5 ESV). "Put on then...compassionate hearts, kindness, humility, meekness, and patience" follows "Christ is all, and in all" (3:11-12 ESV). What immediate precedes this new list of husband-wife, parent-child commands is yet one more affirmation of Christ being preeminent in everything:

> And whatever you do, in word or deed, do everything in the name of the Lord Jesus, giving thanks to God the Father through him (3:17 ESV).

Doing *everything in the name of the Lord Jesus* is equivalent to doing everything in Christ. The name of the person *is* the person. When we call a person by name, his name is the tag that identifies who he is. So for us to do everything in the name of the Lord Jesus, that is, in Jesus Himself, is another way of saying He is preeminent in all things. So the command, "Wives, submit to your own husbands, as is fitting in the Lord" and those following, are just as "put to death" and "put on"—outworkings of the preeminence of Christ.

"Husbands, love your wives and do not be bitter toward them." Now here's a specific application of what Paul referred to earlier, "Put on love, which is the perfect bond of unity." A husband can put on love because Christ is all, and in all. As a test of Jesus' preeminence for the wife is submission to her husband, a test for the husband is love for his wife without bitterness. So any time a husband loves his wife with the love of Jesus Christ, it is Jesus Christ loving! It's Jesus exhibiting His preeminence by living the life of love through the husband.

Have you ever been to a marriage seminar or listened to a sermon for married couples and heard, "Wives, submit to your own husbands," and "Husbands, love your wives" quoted out of Colossians? Since the New Testament is frugal in verses explicitly calling out husband-wife relationships, it is highly likely for these verses to have made their way in. Yet how often does the application of these verses omit any mention of the preeminence of Christ developed throughout the letter? Remember that the Holy Spirit originally crafted Colossians as a letter to be read or heard in one sitting. Should the emphasis be on what *you* do as a husband or wife or what *Christ*, in His superabounding eminence, is doing in you?

In our information age with all its wonderful online tools for detailed study at the click of a button, we need to be really careful not to ignore context and unwittingly misinterpret verses, missing the original intent of the author. I know that I have gotten burned many times by not paying close enough attention to the context. Despite our sincere intent to live the Christian life, we can fail miserably in applying the *how to* verses in chapters 3 and 4 by sidestepping their vital connection to chapters 1 and 2.

As we're reading Scripture, it's also really important to distinguish between the author's main point and the *illustration* of his main point. Good illustrations are like windows that let light in, illuminating more abstract thought. Are "Wives, submit to your own husbands," and "Husbands, love your wives" the main points or the sermon illustrations? Paul's grand theme throughout his letter has been the preeminence of Christ. These terse commands inserted into the letter were not intended to be a do-it-yourself instruction manual. If you think about it, there's really not a lot of detailed instruction here. Rather, these serve the grand scheme of things as concrete illustrations to help us envision what Christ's preeminence in all things looks like for different kinds of people in the local assembly.

The main point is not obeying these commands to have a happy marriage or compliant children. A husband loving his wife is Paul's illustration of Jesus living His husband-life of headship through that man; it's Christ expressing His preeminence in all things. Wives submitting to their own husbands, as is fitting in the Lord, is an illustration of what the preeminence of Jesus looks like as it's expressing itself through a wife. A wife can submit to her husband because it's Jesus living (as He lived a life of submission to His Father) through her. The point is that obedience to these commands is evidence that wives, husbands, children, fathers, and bondservants have grasped the message of Colossians chapters 1 and 2.

"Children, be obedient to your parents in all things,

for this is well-pleasing to the Lord" (Colossians 3:20). I've used this verse a lot when working with my kids. I even had my boys memorize it. Though I'm holding out the God's high standard, I also recognize that they are totally incapable of obeying their parents in *all* things until they likewise have embraced the same message of Colossians. That's at the forefront of my mind when I share that verse with my kids.

So how does a child obey his parents in all things? Jesus, who obeyed His earthly parents from birth to adulthood for thirty years, wants to live that life again in children. So when Christ is manifesting His preeminence in a child's life, how does that show itself? The child obeys his parents in all things. A saved kid obeys God's commands the same way that Mom submits to Dad or Dad loves Mom. It's by Christ living in them.

How many times does a child obey his parents through the course of the day? That obedience is not only when he's within eyeshot but anywhere else. So "be obedient...in *all* things" is a signpost drawing attention to the around the clock preeminence of Jesus. God isn't start-stop-start-stop-start-stop in the way He runs the universe. He's not taking coffee breaks while letting the universe run itself. He's continuously involved. "Look at the birds of the air," Jesus asserted, "that they do not sow, nor reap nor gather into barns, and yet your heavenly Father feeds them. Are you not worth much more than they?" (Matthew 5:26). Because God is everlastingly preeminent in creation without intermission, our children—and we—can trust Him to make His Son preeminent for us any time He's needed (which is all the time!).

Now, unsaved children still need the standard of the law and external discipline to lead them to Christ, but a child that's truly died with Christ and been raised with Christ will obey his parents by grace through faith. What if a child who truly knows the Lord is having problems obeying his parents? The solution is not you resorting to lots of rules and regulations. The solution is to show that child his true heavenly identity and what God has done for him in Christ. It's letting him sit down in the easy chair and see in God's scrapbook everything he has in Christ like you do. I know I need this reminder for my oldest child who has faith in Christ; I find it very easy to focus on the commands without bringing the fullness of Christ to bear into her training. Since truly regenerated children have everything they need in Jesus, He can manifest His life in them as well. Christ is "in all," old or young, to those who belong to the kingdom of God. If your child is in Christ, then by faith he or she is to seek the above, where Christ is, seated at the right hand of God.

"Fathers, do not exasperate your children, so that they will not lose heart" (Colossians 3:21). How does a father not exasperate or provoke his child? I know firsthand it's very easy to provoke your children to wrath or discouragement. How do I not do that? Well, it's not by reading twenty-two books on parenting that divert my attention away from Jesus, who is my life. I do enjoy reading parenting books and learn lots of things, but everything I read goes through the filter of the preeminence of Christ that the Lord has taught me in Colossians. You're rooted in Christ and have everything you need in Him. Christ wants to be preeminent in your role as a father. So as you receive Christ, the Son born to you whose name is "Everlasting Father" (Isaiah 9:6), His fatherly life will manifest so you won't provoke your children or cause them to be discouraged.

"Bondservants, obey in all things your masters

according to the flesh, not with eyeservice, as men-pleasers, but in sincerity of heart, fearing God" (Colossians 3:22 NKJV). In our day we don't have slavery like they did in Rome. It was very popular back then. Across the Empire, about one out of ten inhabitants were slaves; in the capital city of Rome, the proportion was one out of two![30] Though slavery is not in vogue today, the principle is still very relevant to our culture. We all have subservient roles we find ourselves in, such as an employee to employer or a subject to governing authorities who promote public welfare and safety, whether the President of the United States or the president of the Home Owners Association. Just as wives are to submit to their own husbands and children are to obey their parents in all things, servants are to obey their masters in all things in the Lord. Why do we obey in all things? It's because Christ in us obeys in all things.

We all know there are exceptions and limitations to authority. If the government asks us to violate God's Law, such as demanding that we lie or steal or murder, that goes outside the boundary of their authority because that's not in the Lord. But things within their jurisdiction that are in the Lord, we obey for the purpose of promoting the preeminence of Jesus in all things. In His desire to very abundantly manifest Christ, God is very pleased to advance His glory in the world.

In the everyday, humdrum life that we live, our obedience to those in authority over us is a test of whether we are being shifted and shaken off the hope of the gospel, the Lord Jesus Christ. If you're a husband, what do you need to do if you're not loving your wife like Christ loves the church? You don't need to implement a bunch of rules to

---

[30] Rodgers, Nigel, *Ancient Rome* (London: Lorenz Books, 2005), p. 258

improve your husbanding. Paul's encouragement is to seek the above, where Christ is, seated at the right hand of God. Christ is seated because the work of redemption is done, so He now sits in the place of manifesting His abundant fullness in you. Do you see that you're raised with Christ? You're one with Him. You have all your life in Christ. "For in him the whole fullness of deity dwells bodily, and you have been filled in him" (Colossians 2:9-10 ESV). What do you need outside of Jesus? It's His performance. He is *the* Husband, manifesting His love in you as you love your wife. He doesn't do it apart from you, but He does it in union with you. That brings Him glory! So none of us can boast or take any credit if we're loving our wives in a godly way.

So how do we live practically as Christians? We live in a vital union with Jesus, our Head, minding what He has done for us, who He is, and who we are in Him. Seek your Savior, from whom life comes. As you keep thinking about Him, that life will automatically and progressively manifest over time. He loves to do it!

Heavenly Father, we're so grateful that Your will is that every Christian have a full Christ to draw from. We are encouraged that You raised us in Jesus and that our life is hid with Him in You. We can put on love because You're giving that freely in Your Son, who is our life. Open our hearts to be pliable and humble to receive. You are the One who gets all the glory for showing Christ in our lives. Everything that's done that brings You praise is because You did it. May Your grace be multiplied to us, we pray, Father, in Jesus. Amen.

CHAPTER 14

Triumphs and Trophies

The doctrinal section of Colossians 1 and 2 emphasize who this Christ is that we've received through hearing the gospel. We've not received law-based and earthbound teachings that are worthless in curbing our fleshly pursuits. Colossians 3 and 4, the daily life application sections, are about walking in Him. So in Colossians 3 we examined how the preeminence of Jesus works itself out in putting off the old man, putting on Christ, and various personal relationships. Paul now moves on from general principles and illustrations to real-life people. We will now see the *principle* of love— "But above all these things put on love, which is the bond of perfection" (Colossians 3:14 NKJV)—*in action* in people. As an example, Epaphras put on love by interceding with deep concern for the saints to stand perfect in all God's will.

We have a tendency to think that the real weighty, meaty stuff in Paul's epistles is at the beginning and middle, but the end is just personal greetings that we can quickly skim over. "So-and-so greets you" just doesn't seem as powerfully relevant as the magnificent preeminence of Christ and the snapshots of awesome grace of the previous chapters. After the Fourth of July fireworks grand finale here in the U.S., we pack up our lawn chairs and head on home. Sometimes we can have that same pack-up-our-stuff-and-go-home mentality with the closing verses of the epistles, thinking the spectacular attraction is over and miss out on precious nuggets of truth hidden in plain sight. There is no barren verse of Scripture, as Paul affirms, for "All Scripture is inspired by God and profitable for teaching, for reproof, for correction, for training in righteousness" (2 Timothy 3:16). So in chapter 4 Paul is not merely concluding the letter with trivialities, like "Aristarchus says hi," but is still locked onto his main theme, further illustrating it with people from everyday life.

God providentially arranged all the circumstances in Paul's life that established his social network with the ten different people listed in the final chapter. His descriptions of these people really clinch the message of Colossians. They embody what faith in Christ preeminent looks like in practice. So it's a very valuable section if we take the time to meditate on it and ask the Lord to give us insight on it. Paul expects his readers to rely on God for a full understanding of his writings. "Consider what I say, for the Lord will give you understanding in everything" (2 Timothy 2:7).

The Pathway to Greater Usefulness
Of the ten different people at the end of his letter, Paul starts off by introducing these two Christian brothers, Tychicus and Onesimus. Tychicus was a seasoned veteran assigned with delivering three letters—this letter, the letter

to Philemon, and the letter to the Ephesians—from Rome all those treacherous miles across land and sea to what is today western Turkey. As we took a deeper dive into Tychicus' life earlier, recall that he was not merely a mail carrier but a trustworthy ministry gift.

> Tychicus, a beloved brother, faithful minister, and fellow servant in the Lord, will tell you all the news about me. I am sending him to you for this very purpose, that he may know your circumstances and comfort your hearts, with Onesimus, a faithful and beloved brother, who is one of you. They will make known to you all things which are happening here (Colossians 4:7-9 NKJV).

The little phrase *in the Lord* (or *in Christ*) has been a big thought through the book of Colossians, not to mention much of the New Testament as well. Tychicus is a "beloved brother, faithful minister, and fellow servant *in the Lord.*" Tychicus and Paul's other friends and coworkers had at one time been sons of disobedience, but the Father had delivered them from the power of darkness and transferred them into the kingdom of the Son of His love. Outside the Lord, they were no different from all these other people Paul spoke of: "Because these things the wrath of God is coming upon the sons of disobedience" (Colossians 3:6). Every child of Adam outside of Christ is a son of disobedience under the power of darkness. So these beautiful character qualities Paul observed—beloved brother, faithful minister, and fellow servant—came as a result of him being in the Lord Jesus.

All of these winsome virtues were the life of the Lord Jesus automatically, freely flowing in his life *consistently.* Tychicus wasn't a beloved brother on Sunday and a scoundrel the other six days of the week. Paul characterized his identity as a beloved brother day in and day out. Those qualities can likewise be ours because Christ is our life, our all and in all. Because Jesus is *the* beloved brother (see Hebrews 2:11), He consistently lives that beloved brother-life in us. The Father wills that Christ be preeminent in our lives like that. In the language of Colossians 3, when God manifested Jesus Christ, Epaphras appeared with Him in glory, a glory expressed as a beloved brother, faithful minister, and fellow servant.

Onesimus was a runaway slave from the Colossae region who somehow ended up in Rome. We know some details about Onesimus' life from Paul's letter to Philemon, his master. We don't how he ended up in prison with Paul, but we do have a record of the transforming power of Christ in his life. Paul wrote to Philemon, "I appeal to you for my child Onesimus, whom I have begotten in my imprisonment, who formerly was useless to you, but now is useful both to you and to me" (Philemon 1:10-11). Here's a guy that was unprofitable and perhaps, as implied by the letter, even a thief. Once a useless, runaway slave, now he's commended as a faithful and beloved brother. Paul prized his usefulness, wishing "to keep [him] with me, so that on your behalf he might minister to me in my imprisonment for the gospel" (1:13). As with Tychicus, the preeminent Christ was appearing in glory through Onesimus.

Compared to Tychicus, Onesimus was a fairly recent convert. Though Tychicus had more longevity, Paul considered both a "beloved brother." So here's Onesimus, a recent believer who's bearing great fruit as a cherished brother. Tychicus had that too, plus he's also immensely profitable in the work of the Lord. As Tychicus' roots grew deeper into Christ, he was even more fruitful as a faithful minister and fellow servant. Be encouraged that as you cling to the Lord Jesus, God makes you more fruitful and useful in His kingdom.

Comfort Personified

As Paul runs down the list of people, he moves from those departing Rome to all those staying back with him.

> Aristarchus my fellow prisoner greets you, with Mark the cousin of Barnabas (about whom you received instructions: if he comes to you, welcome him), and Jesus who is called Justus. These are my only fellow workers for the kingdom of God who are of the circumcision; they have proved to be a comfort to me (Colossians 4:10-11 NKJV).

Aristarchus was probably an early convert from Thessalonica in the Greek province of Macedonia, of which Philippi was the principal city (see Acts 20:4). You can follow a little bit of his story in the book of Acts. Paul enjoyed a real comradery with Aristarchus, his travel companion (Acts 19:29). Near the end of Paul's third missionary journey, this brother had the terrifying experience of being held hostage by a frenzied mob in Ephesus (Acts 19:28-29). Aristarchus was one who literally weathered the storm with Paul. He accompanied Paul en route to Rome in a large ship that a hurricane battered for weeks and eventually shipwrecked. Now he's a fellow prisoner with Paul in the Roman jail. Paul didn't have to do a lot of things alone, because God provided these friends.

Mark is John Mark, the cousin of Barnabas. In Acts 15 Paul and Barnabas had a sharp dispute over Mark because he had deserted them in the first missionary journey. Paul was obviously miffed about it and wanted nothing to do with him coming along for the second missionary journey. Barnabas, the son of encouragement, wanted to give his cousin a second chance. Because they couldn't agree, they parted ways. Eventually Paul came to see eye to eye with Barnabas, for at the end of his life he asked Timothy to "Get Mark and bring him with you, for he is useful to me for ministry" (2 Timothy 4:11 NKJV).

So like Onesimus the runaway slave, John Mark is another triumph and trophy of God's grace. Here's a guy who in Paul's eyes was a useless failure but ended up useful for ministry. We can be certain that Mark is useful because he wrote one of the most popular books in the history of mankind—the Gospel of Mark! God saw fit to use him to chronicle the Lord Jesus' life in a precious Gospel that is permanently included in the Bible.

Mark's usefulness to Paul, along with that of Aristarchus and Justus, is underscored by, "They have proved to be a comfort to me." This is powerful! *Proved* to be a comfort literally is *made* to be a comfort. It's the Greek word *ginomai* (GEH-noh-mahy), the same word used in John 1:3:

> All things were made [*ginomai*] through Him, and without Him nothing was made [*ginomai*] that was made [*ginomai*].

As implied by the passive voice of the verb, God made or created them to be a comfort to Paul! Paul, waiting for trial, had been in very distressing circumstances. Aristarchus, Mark, and Justus were comfort personified, comfort in the flesh. The Greek word for *comfort, paregoria* (par-AY-gor-EE-ah), means a soothing or solace, a cheering relief in sorrow or trouble. This is the only place it is used in the New Testament. W. E. Vine indicates that a verbal form of the noun *paregoria* "signifies medicines which allay irritation." As we're embracing the gospel and receiving Christ, God makes us to be a soothing medicine to afflicted or distressed believers. Because Jesus, as the Consolation of Israel (Luke 2:25), is a comfort, He lives to be comfort in us to those in need. So Christian fellowship is another way of receiving Christ. These other believers made Christ accessible to Paul, causing him to esteem Jesus Christ even more.

If we're in Christ, our fellowship crosses all boundaries. Here Paul is talking about Jews—Aristarchus, Mark, and Justus, "my only fellow workers for the kingdom of God who are of the circumcision." Next he'll be talking about Gentiles—Epaphras, Luke, Demas, and others. Because Christ is all, and in all, there is neither Greek nor Jew, circumcised nor uncircumcised. Just as His fellowship transcends all boundaries made by man, so will ours. No matter what their personalities or racial or denominational backgrounds are, if these people are in Christ, there's a wonderful fellowship that takes place. We share a family bond to support one another that the world doesn't have, because we have Jesus Christ in common.

The Lord's Prayer Life Manifested
Paul spends the most time talking about Epaphras, the pioneer evangelist to Colossae, who's now in jail with him (Philemon 1:21). Here's a guy very much like the apostle Paul who's fervent in prayer, praying always without ceasing.

> Epaphras, who is one of you, a bondservant of Christ, greets you, always laboring fervently for you in prayers,

that you may stand perfect and complete in all the will of God. For I bear him witness that he has a great zeal for you, and those who are in Laodicea, and those in Hierapolis (Colossians 4:12-13 NKJV).

Epaphras has a great zeal or concern for them. Epaphras looks like Jesus here! God put in his heart a great compassion and concern for their souls like Jesus, the Chief Shepherd, has for His sheep. Why does he look like Jesus? As we have been saying, it's because it is Jesus. It is the preeminent Lord Jesus praying in and through him. We see Christ's intercessory ministry through His people, demonstrated by Paul and Epaphras.

Epaphras, our dear fellow servant, who is a faithful minister of Christ on your behalf, who also declared to us your love in the Spirit. For this reason we also, since the day we heard it, do not cease to pray for you (Colossians 1:7-9 NKJV).

The *we* in the Greek is emphatic; the *also* compares their ministry (*do not cease to pray for you*) to that of Epaphras. The *we also* implies that *Epaphras* does not cease to pray for them. Epaphras, therefore, was a minister of intercession, of which chapter 4 leaves no doubt.

In chapter 1, verse 29, Paul referred to his life of preaching and praying, "For this purpose also I labor, striving according to His power, which mightily works within me." Epaphras' fervent laboring in prayer had that same kind of energy in Christ. The Lord Jesus' working in us is what causes our prayers to be fervent.

Epaphras had been a son of disobedience just like everybody else until the amazing power of Christ transformed him from selfish sinner to selfless saint whose mind was focused on God's interests on the earth. He's not praying for fine chariots, the latest fashions in togas and sandals, and all these temporal things. He's praying that they would stand perfect in God's will.

As with Tychicus and Onesimus, there are varying degrees of growth in Christ. Epaphras is a very mature believer in the Lord. We can admire a guy like Epaphras and think, "Wow, I wish I was like that!" I have made the mistake of looking at giants of the faith and trying to imitate them. But this Christian maturity is not accomplished by imitating; it was Christ operating in them and it must be Christ living in us. Epaphras was just an average Joe to whom the Holy Spirit revealed an extraordinary, transcendent Christ. As he faithfully received Christ and wasn't sidetracked by all these other methods and formulas, this preeminent Jesus lived His intercessory life through him. Praying Christians are a manifestation of Christ, who is preeminent in all things. As He conforms us to Himself, being an intercessor like Epaphras and Paul will be the natural byproduct, like apple trees producing apples.

I'm sure Paul could have said much more about Epaphras' life, but this little snapshot serves to illustrate the major message of the letter. His radical prayer life for a handful of local churches is Jesus' worldwide ministry in miniature. We're not unlimited like Jesus. We can't fulfill all the desires of His infinitely big heart, but by His working we can bear our allotted fruit in our little corner of His vineyard. Just flow in the current of His Spirit who makes us sensitive to the real interests of the heart of God.

The Beloved Physician
It intrigues me that Mark, Luke, and Paul who penned much

of our New Testament[31] are here. With two of the four Gospel writers present with Paul in Rome, what a solid reminder for him to stay on target with the gospel, not to be shifted or shaken off Christ whom he'd originally received.

> Luke the beloved physician and Demas greet you (Colossians 4:14 NKJV).

Paul calls Luke *the beloved physician*. Jesus, of course, is *the* beloved Physician. The Lord is occasionally addressed using everyday occupations, such as carpenter (Mark 6:3) and shepherd (John 10:11). Luke recorded Jesus as saying, "Those who are well have no need of a physician, but those who are sick" (Luke 5:31 NKJV). In Doctor Luke "beloved" and "physician" are combined. This unique blending has shaped my thoughts and prayers about the Lord Jesus as not only a healer but a beloved physician.

What's neat about Luke is that he remained faithful to Paul to the end.

> Be diligent to come to me quickly; for Demas has forsaken me, having loved this present world, and has departed for Thessalonica—Crescens for Galatia, Titus for Dalmatia. *Only Luke is with me.* Get Mark and bring him with you, for he is useful to me for ministry. And Tychicus I have sent to Ephesus (2 Timothy 4:9-12 NKJV).

So Luke, along with Tychicus and Mark, remained true right up to the end of Paul's life. Luke staying true to

---

[31] Of the 138,020 Greek words in the Analytical Greek New Testament (AGNT), these three have about 59% of the total. Luke has 37,933, Paul 32,407, and Mark 11,304, as reported by http://apologika.blogspot.com/2014/05/who-wrote-most-of-new-testament.html (retrieved March 17, 2016).

the end reminds us of Jesus, the beloved Physician who will faithfully stay with us to the end. "Lo, I am with you always, even to the end of the age" (Matthew 28:20). As Luke continued embracing the message of Colossians, the appealing trait of beloved physician radiated from his life as a shining ray of the Lord Jesus.

The Head disperses life to each individual member in the body. When the hand is in union with the head, it becomes a faithful hand, and that brings glory to the Master. We may not have the gift of beloved physician as Luke, but we are all called to be in some way, shape, or form a part of Christ's body to glorify Him. He *will* be consistently preeminent as we just give ourselves in faith to Him as presented in the gospel.

Demas, in contrast with Luke (and his other eight contemporaries listed here), has a colorless reference here in Colossians. Nothing is said about him other than the bare mention of his name. He had a name of renown but apparently no life. Perhaps Paul's omission of anything praiseworthy about Demas was a foreboding of his full-blown heart for the world later on. Unlike Luke, Tychicus, and Mark, Paul relayed the bad news that "Demas, having loved this present world, has deserted me" (2 Timothy 4:10). Demas rejected the message of Colossians of receiving Christ, replacing it with receiving the world. No man can serve two masters.

Take Heed to the Ministry

> Now when this epistle is read among you, see that it is read also in the church of the Laodiceans, and that you likewise read the epistle from Laodicea. And say to Archippus, "Take heed to the ministry which you have

received in the Lord, that you may fulfill it." This salutation by my own hand—Paul. Remember my chains. Grace be with you. Amen (Colossians 4:16-18 NKJV).

We don't know much about Archippus other than this reference and his being mentioned in Philemon as "a fellow soldier." The fact that Archippus is in Laodicea is intriguing, because we know from Revelation 3 years later that this became the lukewarm church where Jesus stood knocking outside the door. He may have been one of the leaders in that church. But whatever he was, Paul ends with a principle that applies not only to Archippus but to every Christian: "Take heed to the ministry which you have received in the Lord, that you may fulfill it."

How do we fulfill any ministry that God has given us? It's *in the Lord*. We fulfill ministry as Tychicus did as a "fellow servant *in the Lord*." Archippus' faithfully fulfilling that ministry was *in the Lord*. Unfulfilled ministry may be an indication that we're drifting from the message of Colossians. So we need to go back to chapters 1 and 2 and go upstairs to see our colossal Christ. We will be faithful in our ministry if we are faithful to our first ministry, which is receiving Christ, our first love. Our first ministry is what Jesus calls one thing needful:

Martha, Martha, you are worried and troubled about many things. But one thing is needed, and Mary has chosen that good part, which will not be taken away from her (Luke 10:41-42 NKJV).

Mary is commended for having chosen the one thing that's needful, and that's receiving Him by sitting at His feet and receiving what He has to say. Satan wants to get us sidetracked from staying true to this *one thing*. He has lots of ways to divert our attention and blind us to the glory of Christ (2 Corinthians 4:4).

So as we finish up Colossians, how do we gain Christ? It's by taking heed to the message, the good news. We don't need other messages to supplement the gospel because Christ is our all-sufficiency. If we stay put on that, we will be glorious examples of what our colossal, preeminent Christ does. John Mark, useless turned useful, may have learned this from his Uncle Barnabas.

> When [Barnabas] came and had seen the grace of God, he was glad, and encouraged them all that with purpose of heart they should continue with the Lord. For he was a good man, full of the Holy Spirit and of faith (Acts 11:23-24 NKJV).

If you had only one message to inculcate spiritual growth for new believers, what would you say? The Holy Spirit, who filled Barnabas, urged them to continue with the Lord Jesus, the theme running through the book of Colossians. As you started with the Lord, continue steadfastly with the Lord.

CHAPTER 15

Practically Seeking the Above

The aged apostle, detained in a Roman prison, was on a mission from God: to encourage the discouraged disciples in Colossae. Paul's strategy not only included praying for them, but presenting the preeminence of Jesus Christ in an inviting, captivating way. In the practical second half of his letter, he shows how God sculpts godly character and wholesome relationships out of the marble slab of Christ's preeminence. The grand finale is living and breathing sculptures of real-life people who exhibit what lives look like when they're not shaken off the hope of the gospel but are still holding fast to the Head.

My wife's artistic flair finds an outlet in cooking for friends and family. Marian loves cookbooks, but only if there are pictures. She has to visualize the finished product before the recipe can inspire her to act. The fruitful service of Tychicus, the incarnation of comfort in Aristarchus, Mark, and Justus, and the electrifying prayer life of Epaphras are all pictures to inspire us to act by faith to lay hold of a preeminent Christ.

Several chapters ago, we took a deep dive into the meaning of the things above.

> Keep seeking the things above, where Christ is, seated at the right hand of God. Set your mind on the things above, not on the things that are on earth (Colossians 3:1-2).

The things above, literally "the above," boil down to the heavenly message of the gospel of Christ. *The things that are on earth*, or "the below," were those teachings that abandoned Christ, clinging rather to the earthly, preparatory principles—food and festival observances, law-keeping, and rule following. The false teachers had it all turned upside down: "If you have the laws, you'll have a glorious life." Paul refuted that, contending, "You'll never get it that way. Christian life is obtained through holding fast to the Head, Christ Jesus the Lord, who is your life." Paul's final assessment of these so-called "wise" teachings was that they had no value in overcoming the indulgence of the flesh, the very prize the Colossians sought to obtain.

To seek and set our minds on the above is a healthy passion for seeing Christ unveiled from the gospel. What's thrilling for us is that the gospel is where we encounter Christ! Our receiving Christ Jesus Himself, as it was in the beginning, happens as we continue hearing and believing God's word. We don't search the Scripture for eternal life in and of itself, but approach it as a signpost that points to Jesus (see John 5:39-40). We pay attention to who Christ is and what He has done for us—surveying God's scrapbook of Colossians 1 and 2. When Christ, not our spiritual performance, occupies the landscape of our mind, that's when we actually experience the "constantly bearing fruit and increasing" in daily life. This is so counterintuitive to the deeply ingrained thinking that rewards come from our good behavior.

Since seeking the above, where Christ is, sitting at the right hand of God, is of such paramount importance, how do we do that? If all we need is Jesus, how do we practically appropriate His life? Fortunately for us, Paul is a very practical guy when it comes to theology. Throughout Colossians he points out several down-to-earth ways we can seek the above in order to receive this awesome, colossal Christ each and every day.

Seeking the Above: Preaching and Fellowship
The most obvious way of seeking the above is the way we experienced Christ at the very beginning—through the gospel. Paul attributes the Colossians' early successes in faith and love to Epaphras' gospel teaching.

> Of this you have heard before in the word of the truth, the gospel...*just as you learned it from Epaphras* our beloved fellow servant (Colossians 1:5, 7).

When the Colossians first set their minds on the above, the gospel they learned from Epaphras, that's when they received Christ Jesus the Lord.

> Therefore, as you received Christ Jesus the Lord, so walk in him, rooted and built up in him and established in the faith, *just as you were taught*, abounding in thanksgiving (Colossians 2:6-7).

The gospel, *just as you were taught*, is the common denominator of their initial experiences in grace and their ongoing experiences in grace. Christ, the object of your faith when you were first taught, is still the same object of faith in your walk in Him. So fruitfulness begins by trusting in Christ and continues by trusting in Christ. This Bible-based teaching that we first received is *the above* that we are to regularly give our thoughts and affections to. Our spiritual walk is maintained by habitual, repeated gazes at Jesus in the gospel, which we pointed out earlier refers to any portion of Scripture that unveils Jesus.

As with all of Paul's letters, Colossians deals with spiritual realities, not necessarily how things appear. Paul sees beyond the earthly instrument, Epaphras, to God who does all the real work. Epaphras is just a supporting actor who's eclipsed by the heroic superstar, God, who rescued them from the kingdom of darkness. So when these believers first set their minds on the above, the word of grace they were taught by Epaphras, *God* gave them His Son! Paul affirms the same principle elsewhere:

> I planted, Apollos watered, but God was causing the growth. So then neither the one who plants nor the one who waters is anything, but God who causes the growth (1 Corinthians 3:6-7).

Do you want to know where to find God powerfully at work today? It's through people like Paul, Apollos, and Epaphras. It's through the pastor of the local church faithfully tending to the message of Jesus Christ and Him crucified. It's through Christ-centered teachers through their messages on television, radio, or the Internet or through Christ-centered authors in their books or blogs. Our gospel diet, though, isn't restricted to the specially gifted pastors, teachers, evangelists, or theologians. It's through brothers and sisters in Christ who disciple you or encourage you in the Lord. Fellowship with your run of the mill brothers and sisters in Christ can also function in a similar way, as we share what we heard fresh about Jesus together. Paul's relationships with other believers, as we observed in the previous chapter, increased his prizing of Jesus Christ.

So taking in gospel preaching or teaching, reading and meditating on Scripture, and fellowship are practical ways to powerfully set our minds on the truth of God that rivets our attention on Jesus.

Seeking the Above: Praying

Another practical example Paul offers on how we are to seek the above is prayer. Paul's opening prayer appeals to God to open their understanding of His will.

> And so, from the day we heard, we have not ceased to pray for you, asking that you may be filled with the knowledge of his will in all spiritual wisdom and understanding, so as to walk in a manner worthy of the Lord, fully pleasing to him, bearing fruit in every good work and increasing in the knowledge of God (Colossians 1:9-10 ESV).

The basic thoughts are two-fold. First, Paul prays that these believers might be filled with the knowledge of God's will. The second thought flows out of the first. Knowing God's will, in addition to increasingly knowing God better, leads to *bearing fruit in every good work.* This prayer that they might *walk in a manner worthy of the Lord, fully pleasing to him,* aligns with the key verse of the whole letter: "Therefore, as you have received Christ Jesus the Lord, so walk in Him" (Colossians 2:6). Paul believed that the Colossians' walking in Him, walking in a manner worthy of the Lord, was advanced through his unceasing prayer for them to be filled with the knowledge of God's will. Epaphras' prayers carry the same burden:

> Epaphras, who is one of you, a bondservant of Christ, greets you, always laboring fervently for you in prayers, that you may stand perfect and complete in all the will of God (Colossians 4:12).

How are you going to stand perfect and complete in all the will of God? Your perfection goes back to Paul's assertion, "Him we preach, warning every man and teaching every man in all wisdom, that we may present every man perfect [mature, complete] in Christ Jesus" (Colossians 1:28 NKJV). Though Paul has asserted that we are full in Christ, that fullness is not without limitations. What we are not full of is the knowledge of His will in all spiritual wisdom and understanding. So while we have already been given everything in Christ and *are* full, what we lack is spiritual eyesight to see it. Ed Miller has often remarked, "What we need is eyes to see what we already have in Christ."

So what was God's will that Paul and Epaphras prayed about so fervently? That's what this whole letter is about. God's will is His willingness to make Jesus Christ preeminent for every need, that we would find everything in Him. God's will is that you wouldn't look to any other source except Jesus, whom He freely gives you. We might paraphrase their prayers like this: "Father, open their eyes to see how willing You are to make Christ preeminent in their lives so they can walk before You in a worthy way." As preeminent as God made Jesus in the universe, He delights to make Him readily accessible and continuously preeminent in our lives, every moment of the day. Having God's will firmly fixed in our minds like this counteracts the subtle tactics of the enemy to erode confidence in Christ by having us think that He's great, just not everything we need. So in your steadfast continuing in seeking the above in God's word, be seeking the Father's spiritual wisdom and understanding to show you Jesus and what you already have in Him.

How different are Paul's and Epaphras' prayers than my prayers often have been or the typical prayer requests in Christian circles—pray for so-and-so who's sick, someone lost a job, someone has a marriage problems or difficulties with children. Now, it's great to look to the Lord in our times of need. We should do that. But perhaps we need to reprioritize what our greatest need is—becoming familiar with God's will, understanding who His Son is, and who we are in Him. What also strikes me about Paul and Epaphras is that their continuous fervency conveys that they really believed that people's lives would be changed because they prayed. When we pray in faith for people to be more conformed to Jesus, God is answering those prayers.

We were once dead in our sins and trespasses. We used to walk in ways like fornication, uncleanness, passion, evil desire, and covetousness, which is idolatry. When we received Christ, our all in all, He overwhelmingly set us free from those sinful bondages we used to love and enabled us to have a vibrant prayer life. Yet, in spite of all this, a common lament among Christians is a lackluster prayer life. "My prayer life is really weak and kind of dwindling and fizzling." If we're not continuing earnestly in prayer with thanksgiving, the solution is not to attack it like a New Year's resolution by enrolling in some kind of prayer program, following strict guidelines, or imitating people of prayer. I've been in all those kind of bondages. Very early in my Christian life I experimented with a book by Larry Lee called *Could You Not Tarry One Hour*? Okay, set your clock and give yourself one hour of prayer. That didn't go very far for me. After fifteen minutes I ran out of things to say and spent the remaining forty-five minutes clock watching. It was just a frustrating, legalistic attempt of me trying to make my Christian life happen.

Years ago before this message of Colossians became real to my heart, I periodically felt guilty that I wasn't praying night and day for others like Paul did. So I tried to imitate Paul by praying more late at night, and it seemed to work—for a little while. But like all old covenant obedience, once I turned my attention off that imitation, it too faded away as did the shine on Moses' face (see 2 Corinthians 3:13 NASB). But as my focus turned more and more to Jesus, my prayer life has become more automatic, responding to the promptings of His Spirit throughout the day.

If you have an anemic prayer life, that's just an indicator for you to go back to chapters 1 and 2. Go through the divine scrapbook to let your mind dwell on how great Christ is, what He has done for you, and who you are in Him. See that He is your life. In Christ is all the fullness of the Godhead bodily, and you are full in Him. As your mind is ablaze with these glorious truths, God will reveal Christ, the hope of glory, to you as your all in all. He will increasingly perfect your prayer life as an expression of your preeminent High Priest interceding through you. The preeminence of Christ will manifest automatically to tune our hearts to be thank-filled intercessors for others, as He is.

Seeking the Above: Singing

Besides absorbing our minds with God's word pointing to Christ and praying with thanksgiving for spiritual understanding of God's will, Paul also calls attention to singing as a way of seeking the above. In the church back in

Paul's day were a lot of uneducated Roman slaves, so singing was one effective method for the illiterate to set their mind on written truth. We do this today for children who can't read yet but can learn songs like "Jesus Loves Me." It's hard to imagine in twenty-first century America, with multiple Bibles in our homes, to realize that it wasn't that way in the church of Colossae. Since hand-copied scrolls of the Scriptures fetched a high price, typically only the wealthy had their own copy. The printing press that made the Bible so cheap and accessible was still 1,400 years off into the future. So believers relied more on songs to set their minds on the above.

> Let the word of Christ dwell in you richly, teaching and admonishing one another in all wisdom, singing psalms and hymns and spiritual songs, with thankfulness in your hearts to God (Colossians 3:16).

Singing Christ-centered psalms, hymns, and spiritual songs can have a powerful effect upon our souls. Notice that the main verb *dwell* is further amplified by the participle *singing* along with fellow participles *teaching* and *admonishing*. In other words, the word of Christ dwelling in us richly comes in conjunction with teaching, admonishing, and singing. So singing is one of the practical ways of setting our minds on the above, or as Paul phrases it here, letting *the word of Christ dwell in you richly*.

Psalms refers primarily to the 150 Psalms we have in our Bible or songs similar to that. We're probably very familiar with hymns that put the great truths of Scripture to music. Spiritual songs might be simple choruses that highlight a particular aspect of God's attributes or Christ's life and work. Singing psalms and hymns and spiritual songs out of a thankful heart to God can be as life-transforming as preaching or praying. This is not to say that songs should take up the front seat of our Christian lives, but should be a great supplement to hold fast to the Head, Jesus.

Singing has a unique, unforced way of expressing and repeating the word of Christ to our souls. Who can calculate the inestimable good that has come to the church from hymns such as John Newton's "Amazing Grace"?

> Amazing grace how sweet the sound
> That saved a wretch like me
> I once was lost but now am found
> Was blind but now I see

I love hymns. I love to sing them and even at times to read through a hymnal to set my mind on the above through the richness of truth compacted in each stanza. Another one of my favorite hymns that resonates with "[God] having forgiven us all our trespasses" (Colossians 2:13) is "Jesus Paid It All":

> Jesus paid it all
> All to Him I owe
> Sin had left a crimson stain
> He washed me white as snow

In the universal church today, it's beautiful to see that when Christ is the central focus, the theological background of the hymn writer fades away. There's the big battleground that's been around for centuries between the Arminian (man's responsibility) and Calvinistic (God's sovereignty) points of view. People can enjoy hymns from writers of these polarized theological perspectives in the Christian faith, whether a Charles Wesley ("Come, Thou Long Expected Jesus") from the Arminian persuasion or an

Augustus Toplady ("Rock of Ages Cleft for Me") from a Calvinistic point of view. Now there's a big difference between these in-house disputes and what these false teachers that Paul contended with were doing. Had the false teachers in Colossae written their own songs and hymns, their content would have been setting one's mind on the below. Obviously Paul has in mind these kind of hymns that have Christ as the center.

In different worship gatherings I have noticed that some songs focus more on what *we* do for God than on what *God* does and has done for us. Songs like "I love You, Lord" that express our response to Him definitely have their place. But Christ-centered music, highlighting the excellencies of Jesus Christ's person and finished work, makes me joyful and lighthearted, lifting me out of discouragement or apathy. Knowing that singing is another practical way of setting our minds on the above to encounter Christ Himself should really transform our private and corporate worship, heightening our expectation, participation, and adoration.

Ephesians addresses singing from a slightly different angle:

> But be filled with the Spirit, addressing one another in psalms and hymns and spiritual songs, singing and making melody to the Lord with your heart (Ephesians 5:18-19).

Whereas Colossians emphasizes singing in connection with the word of Christ dwelling in us richly, Ephesians stresses it as an outworking of being filled with the Holy Spirit. Together they form the inseparable bond of word and Spirit. The Spirit glorifies the Lord Jesus from the word. As we sing heartfelt psalms and hymns and spiritual songs, the Spirit is actually at work to set our minds on the above—the free and rich pronouncements of what Christ has done for us. When we see Jesus as the Spirit-glorifying word of God reveals Him, we are being transformed into the same image of our Lord (2 Corinthians 3:18).

As a word of caution, though, you can sing all these songs in a way that alienates you from the transforming life of Jesus. Songs, whether in our Sunday gathering or alone at home or elsewhere, are wonderful God-given means with which we can touch the Lord, but it requires faith. Recall the woman of faith with an issue of blood for twelve years.

> And a woman who had a hemorrhage for twelve years, and could not be healed by anyone, came up behind Him and touched the fringe of His cloak, and immediately her hemorrhage stopped. And Jesus said, "Who is the one who touched Me?" And while they were all denying it, Peter said, "Master, the people are crowding and pressing in on You." But Jesus said, "Someone did touch Me, for I was aware that power had gone out of Me" (Luke 8:43-46).

A lot of folks touched the garment but never touched the heart of Jesus. Faith goes past the garment to touch Jesus. In the corporate worship setting, many people can be singing the same song, but the heart-knowing Lord is sensitive to genuine faith behind the words. Faith goes past the psalm, hymn, or spiritual song to touch Jesus.

Pastor and theologian John Piper has a great illustration about glorifying God that fits well to the corporate means of grace during singing psalms, hymns, and spiritual songs.

> A fountain is not glorified by us hauling buckets of dirty water up the mountain and pouring them in. A

fountain—a spring in a mountain—is glorified, rather, by us lying down at the edge of the stream, putting our face in, drinking our fill, and getting up and saying, "Ah!" That's called worship.[32]

Can a fountain be glorified? Yes, by coming and drinking. The glory of the fountain is that it fulfills the purpose for which it was created. God's original purpose for man in His image was to be a receiver. When sin turned everything upside down, man thought of himself as the giver, not the receiver. God wills that we be completely satisfied by receiving His Son. Paul does a lot of theological heavy lifting through two chapters to get us to see God's scrapbook of everything He did for us in Christ. As we set our mind on the above by Scripture study and meditation, focused prayer, fellowship, or praise and worship, our willing Father reveals His Son to us, liberating us from the power of indwelling sin and radiating His glory through us. As drinking glorifies the water fountain, so we glorify Him by receiving. In this new creation, God has uniquely fashioned your heart to receive Christ, to be a temple where He can settle down and be at home. "As you have received Christ Jesus the Lord, so walk in Him."

---

[32] Piper, John, "Can We Give Anything to Christ?," December 26, 2007 (retrieved from http://www.desiringgod.org/interviews/can-we-give-anything-to-christ)

CHAPTER 16

Our Share of the Inheritance

Throughout Colossians Paul has endeavored to buttress our assurance that everything we need for a God-pleasing life is in the Lord Jesus. The key verse we've investigated is "Therefore as you have received Christ Jesus the Lord, so walk in Him" (Colossians 2:6). So Colossians 1 and 2 speak of how awesome this Christ whom you have received is. He's the magnificent Creator and Redeemer, reconciling all things to Himself, the beginning, the firstborn from the dead, that in everything He might be preeminent. All of us who have believed in the Lord Jesus have also received an inheritance, as Colossians 1:12 reveals, "Giving thanks to the Father, who has qualified us to share in the inheritance of the saints in Light." What is this inheritance? Is it heaven or treasures in heaven? Eternal life? The kingdom of God? A mansion in glory? No, our Sunday school catch-all answer, "Jesus," will do here. Considering that Paul's theme has been the preeminence of Jesus, it should not come as any surprise that our inheritance in Light is our Lord Jesus Christ, too.

Every Christian is filled in Christ. "For in him the whole fullness of deity dwells bodily, and you have been filled in him" (Colossians 2:9-10 ESV). When you received Christ for the first time, you received a full Christ. The Lord Jesus is not divvied out like pieces of an apple pie at a church potluck dinner. You have been filled in Him who is the treasury of the fullness of the Godhead. Romans 8:32 declares, "He who did not spare His own Son, but delivered Him over for us all, how will He not also with Him freely give us all things?" Everything we have that has true value in God's eyes is in His Son. "Blessed be the God and Father of our Lord Jesus Christ, who has blessed us with every spiritual blessing in the heavenly places in Christ" (Ephesians 1:3). Every Christian has been united to Him and has all of the inheritance.

But it begs the question, "If we all have all of Christ, why do some seem to have more of Christ?" I mean, we see these spiritual giants in Christendom like Polycarp, Augustine, Martin Luther, John Wesley, Jonathan Edwards, William Carey, Charles Spurgeon, Hudson Taylor, George Muller, D. L. Moody, Smith Wigglesworth, Corrie Ten Boom, Jim Elliot, and Billy Graham, just to name a few. And we notice that we as fellow believers do not seem to partake of Christ our inheritance to the same degree.

If we all have Christ as our inheritance and all of Christ is available to us, how do we appropriate Him? How do we more fully enjoy Christ as our inheritance? We have already seen how Paul provided several practical tips on seeking the above, such as paying attention to Scripture, prayer, fellowship, and singing. By engaging our hearts and minds in these activities, with the goal of seeing by faith the glory of Christ, we do appropriate the fullness of the Lord Jesus that is already ours. Here it is helpful to consider how the Old Testament accounts of Israel's history foreshadow the fullness of our inheritance in Christ.

Foreshadows of the Greater Victory

In his letter to the Colossians, Paul makes a few allusions to the Old Testament. He shows how redemptive history, aspects of Israel's past that point to Christ's redeeming work, is spiritually relevant for the New Testament people of God. Colossians and the rest of Paul's letters explain the historical events in Israel's far-reaching history of ups and downs, culminating in the appearance of their long-awaited Messiah. Paul has also interpreted the factual accounts of Jesus' life, death, burial, resurrection, and ascension to demonstrate their redemptive applications for the people of God. For example, the death of Jesus has an implication that we also died with Him, thereby freeing us from the tyranny of sin and liberating us from the commandments of men (Colossians 2:20-21). In one broad stroke he has summed up the entire ceremonial law with all its intricacies and fine print as shadows whose substance is Christ:

> Therefore no one is to act as your judge in regard to food or drink or in respect to a festival or a new moon or a Sabbath day—things which are a mere shadow of what is to come; but the substance belongs to Christ (Colossians 2:16-17).

In one of his recorded sermons, Paul encapsulates Israel's history in Exodus and Joshua:

> The God of this people Israel chose our fathers and made the people great during their stay in the land of Egypt, and with an uplifted arm He led them out from it....When

He had destroyed seven nations in the land of Canaan, He distributed their land as an inheritance (Acts 13:17, 19).

Paul condenses the themes of Exodus—deliverance—and Joshua—inheritance—into these two verses in Colossians:

> Giving thanks to the Father, who has qualified us to share in the inheritance of the saints in Light. For He rescued us from the domain of darkness, and transferred us to the kingdom of His beloved Son, in whom we have redemption, the forgiveness of sins (Colossians 1:12-14).

God's rescuing us from the domain of darkness is the substance, the reality, of the shadow, the Passover deliverance of the Israelites from the tyranny of their Egyptian captors. Charles J. Rolls interprets it this way:

> The lesser triumph of the Exodus at the crossing of the Red Sea foreshadowed the greater victory of emancipation achieved by Christ at the Cross for all mankind, a victory over the infernal powers of evil. This also had its memorial throughout all generations. The partial leads us to the perfect, the foreshadow directs to the full substance and the temporal finds its finality in the eternal.[33]

The Old Testament is beautifully illustrated with the *partial*, the *foreshadow*, and the *temporal*—sketches or pictures—until the *perfect*, the *full substance*, and the *finality*—Christ—came. So we look back at Exodus with

---

[33] Rolls, Charles J., *The Indescribable Christ: Names and Titles of Jesus Christ A - G* (Neptune, New Jersey: Loizeaux Brothers, 1983), p. 213

Jesus-glasses on. The Passover lamb with its blood sprinkled on the doorframe of each Israelite home was merely the shadow of which the substance was Christ, as Paul says, "For indeed Christ, our Passover, was sacrificed for us" (1 Corinthians 5:7 NKJV).

Whatever My Lot

Whereas the book of Exodus is about taking the people of God out of bondage, the book of Joshua is about taking them into their promised inheritance. To this we now want to pay attention. Paul's language, "Giving thanks to the Father, who has qualified us to share in the inheritance of the saints in Light" (Colossians 1:12), echoes this grand theme of the book of Joshua. The Greek word for *inheritance, klēros* (KLAY-ros), is literally *lot*, the same word used in the Gospels for the lots the soldiers gambled with to win Jesus' garment. Our modern day equivalent of the lot is rolling dice. This inheritance was not random chance, however, but divinely determined: "The lot is cast into the lap, but its every decision is from the Lord" (Proverbs 16:3). Joshua has six chapters devoted to the use of the lot for distributing the inheritance of the land to the Israelites. So *lot* in the mind of the Hebrew became synonymous with inheritance.

Every kingdom must have at a minimum these three elements: a king, a people, and a land. The kingdom of God in Old Testament times consisted of the king (Jehovah or Yahweh), the people (the circumcised Jews), and the land (Palestine). In the fullness of time, God sent His Son, Jesus Christ, to fulfill promises and prophecies. Now we know that the king, Yahweh, is King Jesus. The people, once depicted primarily as the physical descendents of Abraham, are now the faith-based children of Abraham, which includes Jew and Gentile. That was God's ancient secret that we discussed earlier, an open secret of which Paul was a steward. What about the land, Canaan, the land that flowed with milk and honey? What is this land now in the age of New Testament fulfillment?

We know that the earth is the Lord's and the fullness thereof (Psalm 24:1). We also know from Scripture that Christ, at His second coming, will visibly rule as King of kings over this earth. But what about now? You cannot point to God's kingdom on a world map and say, "Yep, here it is. This is God's kingdom."

I know there are differing views in the body of Christ on this topic, but for the purpose of keeping with the preeminence of Christ in Colossians, we want to explore physical Canaan as the shadow whose substance is Jesus Christ, the true Canaan, our inheritance in Light. He who is king is also the "land" which defines His kingdom. So looking backwards into Israel's history with Christ-glasses on, what was happening in Joshua and Judges was a foretaste of the saints' inheritance in the true and lasting inheritance—Christ Himself.

Moses spoke glowingly of the people's inheritance, the land of Canaan, as a land of abundance and fullness.

> Then it shall come about when the Lord your God brings you into the land which He swore to your fathers, Abraham, Isaac and Jacob, to give you, great and splendid cities which you did not build, and houses full of all good things which you did not fill, and hewn cisterns which you did not dig, vineyards and olive trees which you did not plant, and you eat and are satisfied (Deuteronomy 6:10-11).

This Promised Land is vividly described as a

completed land—finished cities, houses ready to dwell in, cisterns ready to drink from, and mature vineyards and olive groves ready to eat from. For the Hebrew, the land was a promise of fullness. Paul says that Christ now is the fullness and completeness for the Christian. We can give thanks to the Father, the Lord our God, who has brought us into the kingdom of the Son of His love!

The Old Testament has twenty references to the Promised Land as a "land flowing with milk and honey."

> Hence I have said to you, "You are to possess their land, and I Myself will give it to you to possess it, a land flowing with milk and honey." I am the Lord your God, who has separated you from the peoples (Leviticus 20:24).

Milk and honey represent richness, *flowing* abundance. These foreshadow Christ, who is the excellent quality of eternal life that milk and honey convey on a physical plane. The *land flowing with milk and honey* was shorthand for many precious and delightful commodities.

> For the Lord your God is bringing you into a good land, a land of brooks of water, of fountains and springs, flowing forth in valleys and hills; a land of wheat and barley, of vines and fig trees and pomegranates, a land of olive oil and honey; a land where you will eat food without scarcity, in which you will not lack anything; a land whose stones are iron, and out of whose hills you can dig copper. When you have eaten and are satisfied, you shall bless the Lord your God for the good land which He has given you (Deuteronomy 8:7-10).

As we have been saying, the physical pictures the spiritual. The earthly picture is the forerunner to the heavenly reality in Christ. The abundance of water corresponds to its ultimate fulfillment in the living waters, the Holy Spirit, who quenches our thirst with Christ. The abundance of food also finds its final reality in Christ, who is the living bread, the true food, which strengthens His people. The message of Colossians is that we have a Christ in whom we "will not lack anything." Everything we need is in Him. We have been filled in Him. We can bless our God and Father, for the *good land which He has given us*—the Son of His love!

Scripture calls special attention to the inheritance of the tribe of Levi. Unlike the rest, they did not inherit any large parcel of the good land. Rather, their inheritance (apart from some cities to dwell in) was the Lord Himself. In Joshua's day, the inheritances of the Levites and the rest of the tribes were separated. The tribes of Israel got the land flowing with milk and honey; the Levites got the Lord.

> At that time the Lord separated the tribe of Levi to bear the ark of the covenant of the Lord, to stand before the Lord to minister to Him and to bless in His name, to this day. Therefore Levi has no portion nor inheritance with his brethren; *the Lord is his inheritance*, just as the Lord your God promised him (Deuteronomy 10:8-9 NKJV).

In the new and better covenant, both the good land and the Lord as inheritances are united in Christ! The land of milk and honey in its ultimate reality of richness *is* the Lord. The inheritance of the Christian is fantastic beyond all imagination—the fullness of the Godhead bodily! Colossians

3 and 4 take us to the heights of "Mount Pisgah"[34] to survey the panoramic view of our inheritance and its benefits—the defeat of our real enemies (sin and the flesh) and the enjoyment of the kingdom of God—righteousness, peace and joy in the Holy Spirit (Romans 14:17). The richness of our inheritance is the life of Christ—compassionate hearts, kindness, humility, meekness, patience, and love. If you think along these lines, the Colossians' discouragement stemmed from their failure to possess their promised inheritance.

Defeat of Israel's True Enemy
The *put to death* in "Put to death therefore what is earthly in you" (Colossians 3:5 ESV) bears a strong resemblance to the book of Joshua as well. Going in and taking possession of the Promised Land was not a cakewalk. It was filled with enemies—giants and walled cities. The putting to death in this conquest involved Israel in God's judicial prerogatives against the wicked, unrepentant inhabitants of Canaan. God as Judge of all the earth used a flood in Noah's day. At this time, instead of water to bring judgment, He used the sword of this one-of-a-kind theocratic nation. While this might offend the politically correct, we know that God's ways are not our ways. It is His prerogative as Creator and Judge of all the earth to make alive and to kill.

The exodus out of Egypt and the inheriting of Canaan were shadows of the coming good things in Christ. The

---

[34] "Now Moses went up from the plains of Moab to Mount Nebo, to the top of Pisgah, which is opposite Jericho. And the Lord showed him all the land, Gilead as far as Dan, and all Naphtali and the land of Ephraim and Manasseh, and all the land of Judah as far as the western sea, and the Negev and the plain in the valley of Jericho, the city of palm trees, as far as Zoar" (Deuteronomy 34:1-3).

death of the wicked, unrepentant Canaanites in Joshua and Judges foreshadowed the coming good things of the death of Israel's true enemy, which was not Canaanites, Assyrians, Babylonians, Persians, Greeks, or even the Romans. The real enemy was their wayward, wandering heart. See how clearly this is identified for us in Judges:

> Then *the sons of Israel did evil* in the sight of the Lord and served the Baals...So *they forsook the Lord and served Baal and the Ashtaroth*. The anger of the Lord burned against Israel, and He gave them into the hands of plunderers who plundered them; and He sold them into the hands of their enemies around them, so that they could no longer stand before their enemies (Judges 2:11, 13-14).

So internal sin, their doing evil and forsaking the Lord, was why God used the neighboring nations to discipline them. Sin has always been the people of God's number one enemy, not the plunderers. God had to send plunderers to defeat them in order to humble them, convict them of their sin, and bring them to repentance. When the Messiah finally arrived, the people couldn't recognize Him. They sought a deliverer from the Romans rather than a deliverer from their true enemy—sin.

On the flip side, when the armies of Israel went out to battle and won, the victory belonged to the Lord. God made this abundantly clear with their first battle against Jericho, where all the spoils were to be devoted to the Lord. In those days the spoils went to the victor. By devoting the gold and silver and precious things of Jericho to the Lord, He was claiming to be the victor. So the natural eye sees Israel putting the enemies to death, but in reality God is the one delivering the enemies into their hands. So it is in the new covenant. As we studied in a previous chapter, the putting to death of our flesh is directly connected to God manifesting Christ our life and our appearing with Him in glory. So while it is our responsibility to put to death our members which are on the earth to fornication, uncleanness, passion, evil desire, and covetousness, the victory over these enemies is through the power of our preeminent, omnipotent Christ.

Progressive Faith that Glorifies God

If I see some sin operating in my life, this should alert me to come running back to Christ through seeking the above. So if the problems of Colossians 3 are in my life, my thoughts need to return to chapters 1 and 2 to marinate in the gospel, the objective truth of what God has already done for me in Christ. As faith rests in Christ, God willingly and freely manifests His Son. We then appear with Christ in glory, and His power puts sin to death. Our faith in the Lord Jesus brings Him glory. For instance, when we trust Him to be a Savior from our sins, He's glorified in that, for that's what He came to do. So, to the glory of God, faith possesses our inheritance in Christ in all its variety and breadth: Savior, Creator, Shepherd, Messiah, Prophet, Priest, King, Suffering Servant, Baptizer in the Holy Spirit, I am, Bread of life, Vine, Way, Truth, Life, Holy One, Judge, Refiner's Fire, Lord of hosts, Beginning, Morning Star, and many more!

Now through faith *and patience* we inherit the promises (Hebrews 6:12). Sin may be a raging tyrant, but faith looks to the unseen and patiently waits for God to act. Any behavioral change that does not come from the manifestation of Christ to my soul is not real change. It will surely fade away as the glory of Moses' face did under the old covenant. The heart of the old covenant is what I do for

God. The heart of the new covenant is what God does for me in Christ. Paul sums up this contrast in his letter to the Galatians:

> For as many as are of the works of the law are under the curse; for it is written, "Cursed is everyone who does not continue in all things which are written in the book of the law, to do them." But that no one is justified by the law in the sight of God is evident, for "the just shall live by faith." Yet the law is not of faith, but "the man who does them shall live by them" (Galatians 3:10-12 NKJV).

Our strong encouragement, therefore, is to live by faith in what Christ has done for us (e.g., He rescued us from sin and death by His death on the cross) and who answers our every need.

The first time we heard the gospel and trusted in Christ, we received Him in all His fullness. As we continue setting our minds on the gospel, we are not receiving a Christ that we don't already have. "As you have received Christ Jesus the Lord, so walk in Him" points to our need to repeatedly receive Christ, already ours, yet unexplored or not yet fully enjoyed. We began our Christian walk by receiving Christ by faith. We continue our walk the same way: by receiving Christ by faith, little by little, as Israel progressively possessed *their* inheritance:

> I will not drive them out before you in a single year, that the land may not become desolate and the beasts of the field become too numerous for you. I will drive them out before you little by little, until you become fruitful and take possession of the land (Exodus 23:29-30).

Like the progressiveness of the conquests under

Joshua, the judges, and the kings to actual possession and enjoyment of what God had already fully given to them, so it is with us. So our spiritual pilgrimage is not a one-time event, but a continual exploration of the frontiers of Scripture where our guide, the Holy Spirit, freely gives us more of Christ to receive and enjoy.

Problems Downstairs? Go Upstairs!

I hope you now see why I think Colossians is the greatest book on the *how* of holiness in all the Bible. Colossians presents Jesus Christ as the all in all of living a life well-pleasing to the Lord. The simple message of Colossians is that we all possess Christ here and now, not just when we go to heaven.

A pithy one-liner of what it means to seek the above came to mind while I was studying Colossians. I've referred to it several times already. "If you are having problems downstairs, go upstairs." *Upstairs* is the heavenly vision of Jesus Christ and our perfection in Him because of His finished work. Colossians is filled with hope upstairs, unveiling the excellencies of our Lord Jesus and our beautiful relationship with Him as holy, blameless children of God. Our life *downstairs* is our life on this earth that demonstrates whether or not we've grasped our inheritance in Christ. One significant impression Colossians has etched into my soul is a holy habit of running to what Christ has done for me, as highlighted in this verse:

> Yet He has now reconciled you in His fleshly body through death, in order to present you before Him holy and blameless and beyond reproach (Colossians 1:22).

Many times I fall short of my own expectations, my

wife's expectations, my friends' expectations, and others' expectations. Instead of being tempted to despair, I find that my heart has a safety net to keep me from being injured by the criticisms of others. Many times these criticisms are warranted, though their delivery may not make me feel warm and fuzzy. So I "go upstairs" to remind my own heart at that moment that I am holy and blameless and above reproach in the eyes of God. Christ paid the ransom for all my sins and failures, including the one I'm dealing with at the moment. From that wellspring of hope based upon truth that never changes, the Lord alters my attitude and response to one of love instead of sullenness, withdrawal, sarcasm, argument, or some other pet sin to defend my bruised "honor" (pride). During these kinds of tests I have experienced firsthand the grace of God in this holy habit of running to Jesus, the One who presents me before God holy and blameless and beyond reproach and saves me from this present evil age.

On the one side, the glory of Christ manifests as the putting off of the sins of the flesh. On the other side, this glory showcases the true nature of our Lord Jesus in the displaying of His character—love, humility, kindness, mercy. The expressions of these characteristics are Christ. It bears repeating that to the natural eye it looks like us, but the spiritual reality is that it is Christ. "I have been crucified with Christ; and it is no longer I who live, but Christ lives in me; and the life which I now live in the flesh I live by faith in the Son of God, who loved me and gave Himself up for me" (Galatians 2:20).

Thanks for coming along with me on this game-changing journey of the preeminence of Jesus Christ from Colossians! I pray that the Lord will increase your faith and hope in this awesome, colossal Christ to deliver you now from the world, your flesh, and the devil. The Father desires you to enter more fully into your inheritance in His beloved Son. This is a cornerstone for walking in a manner that's worthy of the Lord. Our revolutionary transformation comes as we seek the above, keeping our hearts aligned with the word of truth where the Lord Jesus Christ is ever and always in the spotlight.

The preeminence of Jesus Christ has become an anchor I never had before to keep me from drifting about in a sea of confusing and conflicting distractions, both secular and spiritual. Christ, as firstborn from the dead, wants to be "in all things Himself the one who is preeminent," and that includes you and me! Christ, who is the life, right now is coursing and pulsating through us moment by moment with the same never-ceasing faithfulness with which He maintains every star, planet, and comet in perfect synchronicity in the universe.

Afterword

Nine years have passed since the Lord first dawned on me the preeminence of Jesus Christ in the book of Colossians. It marked a significant turning point for me where God taught me that a whole book of the Bible is all about Jesus. The revelation of our preeminent Lord Jesus Christ from this book has been a conspicuous milestone along my spiritual journey. Colossians is not only God's story but mine, too. The tapestry of my life has been woven with its sacred threads.

There have been many bumps along the way these past nine years to remind me of my need for Christ. Just because God dawns on us the reality of what it means for Christ to be preeminent is no immunity from trials and tribulations in this life. Far from it. The one who penned Colossians also warned, "Through many tribulations we must enter the kingdom of God" (Acts 14:22). Each new trial is a wakeup call—and invitation—that there is still more of Christ my inheritance to possess.

Leaving the church my wife and I had been intimately enmeshed into for nearly two decades, so that we could cling to Christ alone, came with its own baptism of fire—a tarring and feathering by its leadership and an instantaneous loss of all friends and social relationships. Were all the painful trials worth it? Absolutely! "Yet indeed I also count all things loss for the excellence of the knowledge of Christ Jesus my Lord, for whom I have suffered the loss of all things, and count them as rubbish, that I may gain Christ and be found in Him" (Philippians 3:8-9 NKJV). Many more trials exposing my wretchedness have since come and gone to keep me awake to my absolute need for

Jesus. He has been a faithful Shepherd to meet me at every turn and guide me closer to Himself.

For the past eight springs I have attended a men's conference near Lancaster, Pennsylvania, nestled amidst the beautiful forests peppered with Amish, horse-dominated farms. As I have taken prayer walks up and down the trails, I have often reflected on the tall trees that towered above me. Each tree didn't reach that height overnight. It started as a tiny seed and received water, nutrients, and sunshine day after day after day. After many years of this consistent care, the tree becomes a majestic monument to the faithfulness of God. I am hopeful that as I stay rooted in Christ, my soil and and sunshine and rain and everything I need, that at the end I will be as that towering tree. The seed in me is Christ. The mighty redwood I expect is that Christ will be preeminent through me for all to see. May the Lord make us mighty oaks of righteousness as we enjoy more and more seeing Christ unveiled to our hearts in life-transforming ways.

Acknowledgements

There is no way that can adequately thank my Lord Jesus Christ, whom this book is all about. He has been the patient Teacher and faithful Shepherd to guide me through this narrow way.

I have really appreciated the fine-tuned editing skills of Rick Gallipeau, who has made this book a much finer, quality read. His eagle eye for detail along with feedback that helped to better clarify the spiritual content was a real gift of grace.

I am really amazed at how my friend, Jeff Sullivan, picked out the awesome image for the cover and artfully worked the matching fonts. His gracious and willing can-do spirit was refreshing to me.

I'm grateful for how the Lord used my friend, Andrew Park, to be a sounding board that shaped the content and organizational structure in significant ways. After I had begun the process of rewriting this book, I heard what I believed to be the voice of the Lord encouraging me to complete it. Knowing how this would require many months of time commitment, the fleece-seeking Gideon in me asked Him for a confirmation. While at a lunch together, out of the blue Andrew said to me, "You should really publish your studies on Colossians in a book." Wow! I had given the older version to him a number of years prior and hadn't really discussed it since then, so that really confirmed my resolve to complete it.

Finally, I am very thankful to God for ordering my path to cross that of Ed Miller, Bible teacher for Bible Study Ministries, back in early 2006. The Lord has powerfully used his teachings in my life to mentor me by blending diligent scholarship with the indispensable principle of Bible study—

total reliance on the Holy Spirit. On the last day of the men's retreat in Pennsylvania last spring, the Lord showed me a picture in my mind of a candle-lighting service, where one candle after another lights another candle until the once-darkened room is filled with light. God used Ed in my life as a candle that ignited my heart with a passion to see Christ in the Scripture in so many helpful and practical ways. I am very grateful to the Lord for this priceless Christ-centered ministry!

About the Author

Ken Marino grew up in Minnesota and Wisconsin, but has lived in northern Virginia since 1989. A college engineering internship in Virginia was God's opportunity to engineer Ken's salvation in the Lord Jesus Christ. After receiving an Electrical Engineering degree, Ken has worked as a systems analyst in the telecommunications industry for the last two decades.

Ken has a passion for the local church and has served extensively as a leader in various ministries, such as children's ministry, evangelistic outreach, prison/detention center ministry, small group leader, Bible study teacher, and editor of church publications. Ken is thoroughly devoted to seeing Christ in Scripture and has had 8 articles published in a Christian magazine, *A More Excellent Way*.

Ken and his wife, Marian, have three children: Cayla, Josiah, and Micah. Ken enjoys family time, running, reading, travel, personal journaling, hiking, and just about any kind of sweets, especially cheesecake. Ken may be contacted via email at kenmarino@verizon.net.

Made in the USA
San Bernardino, CA
06 April 2016